PSHE
SEX, DRUGS and ROCK 'n' ROLL

PSHE isn't like anything else you do at school...
...because this is stuff you <u>really need to know about</u>.

It's all the important stuff that makes the difference between
you having a nice life — or messing it up.
If you're going to enjoy the life you've got, and avoid the things that
could spoil it for you, then you really need to know the hard facts.

The title <u>PSHE</u> (Personal, Social and Health Education) frankly sounds a bit, well,
"airy-fairy".   Which is a real shame, because this stuff's about as "earthy"
as it gets at school. The fact is this stuff's far more useful to
you (and more relevant) than all the subjects you'll do in your Exams.

That's why we've stuck it all together in one book for you.
We've covered the PSHE curriculum of course, but in a lot of places we've gone
beyond that and put in some of the things they'd never normally tell you — all sorts
of bits and bobs that it's really important you know about.

The key thing with our book is this:
we don't try and tell you how to live your life — all we do is tell you the facts.
After that you'll have to make your own decisions — and live with them.

The truth is, you can live your life in all sorts of different ways, but there's <u>always a</u>
<u>trade-off</u> — whatever you might think, <u>there are no magic solutions</u>.

As someone famous once said...

"Decide what you want — and resolve to pay the price."

Contents

Published by Coordination Group Publications

Contributors:
Simon Cook
Taissa Csáky
Charley Darbishire
Gemma Hallam
Katherine Stewart
With thanks to David Wilson for his help.

ISBN:1 84146 890 8
Groovy website: www.cgpbooks.co.uk
Jolly bits of clipart from CorelDRAW
Printed by Elanders Hindson, Newcastle upon Tyne.
Text, design, layout and original illustrations
© Coordination Group Publications Ltd
All rights reserved.

PSHE is About Real Life

Hope you enjoyed the Sex section. These two pages tell you what PSHE's all about. First off, it's got a little bit more life to it than other subjects. Some people seem to think it's a complete waste of time, but I reckon it's got a few things going for it that most of your other subjects haven't.

PSHE Can Be a Bit of a Laugh

1) PSHE isn't difficult. You don't need to be a super-brain or super-keen, to understand. All you need is a little bit of common sense...

(...but slightly more than this.)

2) There's not much to learn. You probably know most of the stuff in this book anyway — use it to fill in the gaps.

3) PSHE is meant to make your life happier and safer — in other words it should help you enjoy life more.

4) Finding out about sex — and the other stuff — is good old-fashioned entertainment.

PSHE is About Things that Happen to You

Complete Collswallop
MI5 deny semi-colon coverup

Quadratic equations and semicolons don't figure in most people's lives, but I can guarantee there's somebody somewhere in the world having sex, having a drink, smoking a joint, or having a stand-up row (not all at the same time, obviously).

That's the kind of stuff PSHE covers — things that really happen.

The bits about lung cancer or AIDS or suicide aren't meant to scare you. Chances are, most of the bad stuff covered by PSHE won't ever happen to you.

Hopefully though, you'll be a lot less likely to get AIDS or lung cancer if you know how you can get it and how you can avoid it.

It's Impossible to Fail PSHE

The worst thing that can happen to you in a PSHE lesson is that you'll find out something useful — like how not to catch the clap.

There isn't an exam so you can't fail.

At the end of the day, if you'd rather have a long snooze than read this book that's entirely up to you.

PSHE — sex, drugs and rock 'n roll (sort of)...

The main point is that PSHE isn't meant to be a misery or a drag. It should be at least a little bit useful. After all, there aren't that many lessons where you can talk about sex and drugs.

Life Isn't Always Perfect

In an ideal world nothing would ever go wrong. We'd all just float along on waves of loveliness. When things do go bum over boob you need to know who'll be able to give you a hand.

Sometimes You'll Have Big Decisions to Make

1) OK, so every day isn't a long string of life-changing resolutions or moral dilemmas. But sometimes you'll have big or tricky decisions to make.

2) PSHE doesn't tell you what to do — it just gives you some facts. You can take them or leave them.

> *When you're making a decision:*
> *Don't let people bully you into doing anything*
> *you don't really want to do.*
> *Think about all the facts and all the risks involved.*
> *Think about long-term effects as well as short-term,*
> *e.g. fags can give you cancer as well as bad breath.*

You Can't Do Everything On Your Own

1) Most of the time you can think stuff through or sort it out for yourself and you don't need help. But — when you do need help go right ahead and ask.

2) Bottling up your worries about anything is bad. They'll get worse and worse till eventually you can't take any more and you explode.

3) Nobody can help you if they don't know what's wrong.

4) You need to be able to trust people to help you. Sometimes your friends will be able to help. Sometimes you'll need to speak to your parents, a teacher, or another adult — because they've been through things your mates haven't.

Get Help from People who Know Their Stuff

If there's nobody you know who can help, it's time to talk to a professional. Find someone who's an expert at fixing your particular problem. If your telly blows up you don't ask a plumber for help.

1) GPs can deal with health problems, including mental health problems. They can send you to see specialists if you need extra help.

2) The nurse at your surgery will be able to do jabs and some tests for you.

3) Counsellors and therapists talk to you about your problems. It could be a family problem, a drug problem, or something else.

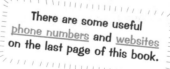
There are some useful phone numbers and websites on the last page of this book.

4) Charities and other organisations can be really helpful with specific problems. e.g. Shelter know all about housing problems. Family Planning Clinics give out free contraception and advice. Most of them have helplines which you can call.

We all need a little help sometimes — just learn to ask...

This is all simple common-sense stuff to make your life easier. You'd be surprised how many solutions there are to the problems you're likely to come up against in your life... and the specialists who've seen it all before really can help — you've just got to ask them.

Knowing the Score

Sex can be <u>fun</u>. It can also be dreadful. This section is about how to <u>enjoy sex</u>. That doesn't mean 'get it on right now' — sometimes the best thing is to <u>wait</u> so you enjoy sex when you do 'do it'.

Sex is Important to People

It doesn't matter if you're <u>having it</u>, <u>not having it</u> or not even that <u>interested</u>. At some point, sex <u>will</u> be <u>relevant</u> to you. Whether you're sexually active or not, there are things you <u>need to know</u> to help you <u>make choices</u>, both now and in the <u>future</u>.

It's best to learn about sex <u>before</u> you start actually making whoopee. <u>Knowledge</u> is <u>power</u>.

No one Wants Bad Sex

Bad sex can be <u>physically painful</u>. Worse than that, the <u>memory</u> of a lousy first time can stay with you for a long time, and make your <u>later</u> sex experience less than heavenly.

Know What You're Ready For

Having sex brings a whole load of <u>consequences</u> along with it. Some of them are <u>physical</u> things, and some of them are more to do with how you <u>feel</u> about yourself.

get set ... go!

1) Obviously, <u>girls</u> can get pregnant.

2) Anyone, <u>boy</u> or <u>girl</u>, can get a sexually transmitted infection.

3) Sex is <u>emotional</u> as well as <u>physical</u>.

Sex isn't just 'penis goes in vagina'. There's far <u>more</u> to being sexual than having <u>standard penetrative sex</u>. Being ready for sexual things like kissing and being ready for <u>penetrative sex</u> are two very different things.

Sort Out Your Own Ideas

There's a lot of <u>rubbish</u> about sex in the media — on **TV** and in magazines. It's as if people think that everyone has to be sexy all the time, and if you're not having it off with a large number of <u>hunky/slinky</u> partners, you're <u>not cool</u>. This is utter <u>cow pie</u>.

No means no

If someone says <u>no</u> to sex, that's what it means. Not 'maybe', not 'perhaps later'. It means 'no'. You need to <u>back off</u>, or risk getting out of your depth and into serious trouble.

Blokes — if you end up <u>having sex</u> after the other person has clearly said <u>no</u>, you could find yourself in court for <u>rape</u> — and that can mean a <u>prison sentence</u>. No excuses will get you out of it. If they said no, and you had sex with them <u>anyway</u>, you could get put away for it.

Just because someone's had sex with <u>other people</u> doesn't mean they've <u>got</u> to have sex with <u>you</u>. Everyone has the right to <u>choose</u> whether or not to have sex with someone.

It doesn't matter whether you're in a relationship or not. Everyone has the right to <u>choose</u> whether or not to have sex <u>every single time</u>.

Whose pants are they, anyway?...

Maybe you don't expect to be getting <u>any sex at all</u>, which is fine. But as soon as you get a new <u>girlfriend</u> or <u>boyfriend</u>, sex can be on the '<u>to do</u>' list quicker than you think. It pays to think ahead.

Deciding When to Have Sex

It's <u>difficult</u> to decide when you're <u>ready</u> for sex. It's not like a huge <u>red light</u> suddenly goes on above your head one day, and that's it, you're ready. <u>Think</u> about it, and bear these things in mind.

Fewer People are Having Sex than You Think

It's easy to think that <u>everyone</u> who's got a boyfriend or girlfriend is having sex <u>all</u> the time.

It's also easy to think that you <u>have</u> to be having sex to prove you're <u>growing up</u>. That's not true. It's totally natural to <u>think</u> about sex loads, but you don't have to prove anything to anyone.

Waiting is Usually Worth It

A lot of people who have sex <u>early</u> can really <u>regret</u> it. Not being <u>ready</u> for your first time makes it <u>rubbish</u>. It's <u>not</u> worth having sex if you aren't going to <u>enjoy</u> it.

And I'm <u>not</u> just talking about regretting it when you're a <u>lot older</u>...

...I mean regretting it the <u>next morning</u> or the <u>next week</u> or when he or she turns out to be a <u>total loser</u>.

Whether it's Yes or No to Sex — it's Up To You

If <u>you</u> feel that sex before marriage is <u>wrong</u>, then you'll probably feel <u>really guilty</u> if you do go ahead and have sex. If your own <u>religion</u> is against sex before marriage, then it's natural that you'll want to do what <u>your beliefs</u> say is right.

<u>No-one</u> has the right to <u>tell</u> you when you should have sex. Your <u>friends</u> <u>don't</u> have the right to make you feel that you <u>ought</u> to be having sex.

It's <u>natural</u> that your <u>parents</u> will feel, at the least, a bit 'icky' about the idea of you having sex. But it is <u>up to you</u>, so don't let them make you feel <u>ashamed</u> of the mere idea of sex. Just don't expect them to be <u>over the moon</u> if you <u>do</u> decide to have sex.

There are Laws about Sex When You're Young

If you have sex with someone <u>under 16</u>, you could end up in trouble with the <u>law</u>. A boy who has sex with a <u>girl</u> under 16 could end up with a <u>criminal record</u>. If he's <u>under 24</u> and he <u>really thought</u> that she was <u>16</u> then he might get away with it, but <u>only once</u>, and only if he's very lucky.

The police take it <u>much more seriously</u> if you have sex with a girl under 13. <u>Prison sentences</u> are actually quite likely. Society really doesn't like this — even if you're a young lad yourself.

<u>Gay men</u> who have sex where <u>other people</u> might see them can find themselves in trouble with the law if they're found out.

If a <u>teacher</u> has a <u>sexual relationship</u> with a <u>pupil</u> under 18 — it doesn't have to be full sex — the <u>teacher</u> can get into <u>very serious trouble</u>.

Waiting's great — waiters are sooooo good looking...

There's no real <u>hurry</u>. Sex won't <u>cease to exist</u> if you decide to <u>wait</u> for a bit. The important thing is being ready when you eventually go for it. Then there's the <u>legal stuff</u> — mostly just common sense.

What You Want From Sex

Knowing what <u>you</u> want from sex is important.

People want Different Things out of Sex

There are lots of <u>different</u> ways of <u>giving</u> and <u>sharing</u> sexual pleasure with someone.

People look for all sorts of <u>different things</u> from sex. Some people want a <u>quickie</u>, some people want a <u>cuddle afterwards</u>, some people want a <u>totally mindblowing</u> experience where the earth moves and two <u>souls meet</u> in <u>perfect harmony</u> (or something like that, so I've heard).

What Men Want

There is <u>no</u> 'what men want'.

Some people think men <u>have</u> to want <u>penetrative sex</u> <u>all</u> the time. That <u>isn't</u> true.

Boys and men can be <u>more</u> interested in sex at <u>some</u> <u>times</u> than at others. It depends on the person.

There's <u>no law</u> that says you <u>have</u> to be <u>wanting</u> sex all the time (and <u>getting</u> it all the time) to be a <u>man</u>.

Men need <u>caring</u> relationships, and <u>closeness</u>, and <u>cuddling</u>, and all that sort of thing.

What Women Want

There is <u>no</u> 'what women want', either.

Some people think that women want relationships and don't <u>really</u> want sex. That <u>isn't</u> always true, either.

Girls and women can have <u>strong sexual feelings</u>. What a girl wants depends on that <u>individual girl</u>.

Think about it like this:
men and women also like cake. Not all men, not all women, obviously — just most people.

There are some Bad Reasons to Have Sex

1) People want to <u>feel loved</u>. Having sex won't help — love can go with sex, but it doesn't <u>always</u>.

2) Some people have sex to <u>keep</u> a <u>boyfriend</u> or a <u>girlfriend</u>. A <u>relationship</u> is about a whole lot <u>more</u> than sex. A good boyfriend or girlfriend will understand if you want to wait.

It's only a drink, Bob. It doesn't mean anything.

3) Some people have sex because they feel they <u>owe</u> it to someone. Sex isn't something you <u>can</u> owe. Buying someone a <u>drink</u> or taking them out on a <u>date</u> does not give you the right to have <u>sex</u> with them.

4) Some people have sex to feel that they've got <u>power</u> over someone. This isn't what sex should be about. Sex is about <u>sharing</u>, not <u>winning</u> and <u>losing</u>. If you want to <u>play games</u>, get a Playstation.

5) Some <u>boys</u> have sex with <u>girls</u> to prove they aren't gay. That's <u>ridiculous</u>. If you're <u>straight</u>, you're straight, and you don't have to <u>prove</u> it. If you're <u>gay</u>, you're gay — and you'd still be <u>capable</u> of having sex with a girl even if you <u>hated</u> it.

You're <u>only</u> gay if you <u>only</u> want to have sex with people the <u>same sex</u> as you. <u>One-off</u> unpleasant sex with someone of the opposite sex <u>doesn't</u> make you gay.

You can't find out that you're <u>loved</u>, <u>attractive</u>, or <u>popular</u> from a quickie behind the gym, or from drunk sex at a party. Friends and <u>good relationships</u> can make you feel <u>loved</u>. <u>Bad sex</u> just <u>can't</u>.

Give us an S! Give us an E! Give us an X!...

Basically it's a <u>bad plan</u> to have sex just for the sake of what <u>other people</u> think. You're more likely to <u>regret</u> it if you do it for a stupid reason. Don't let anyone <u>bully</u> you or <u>manipulate</u> you into it.

Myths and Worries about Sex

When puberty's <u>over</u> you might worry that you're not <u>normal</u> and now it's too late to change.

You're Almost Certainly Normal

Gentlemen — a <u>small penis</u> isn't the <u>end</u> of the world.

There's a lot less variation in size with <u>hard</u> penises than <u>soft</u> ones. 90% of penises are between 14 and 18 cm long when they're hard.

Vaginas have got some <u>muscle tone</u>, so don't worry, it won't feel like you're pushing a pencil up Regent Street if and when you do have sex with a woman. Remember, a vagina can <u>tightly</u> hold something as <u>small</u> as a <u>tampon</u>, and let something as large as a baby out.

Most men have one <u>testicle</u> larger than the other. The testicles tend to hang at slightly <u>different heights</u> (it helps stop them <u>banging together</u> when you walk).

Katy's rucksack was not heavy enough to prevent her from falling over.

Ladies — <u>breasts</u> aren't everything. A lot of boys don't <u>actually</u> think big breasts are that important. They just <u>pretend</u> to, because they think that's the way it <u>ought</u> to be. Stupid, really.

Most women have one breast ever so slightly <u>larger</u> than the other. If one was the size of a <u>brussels sprout</u> and the other was the size of a <u>watermelon</u> it'd be OK to worry. Otherwise, you're normal. They'll even out in time, anyway.

Also, a lot of women have <u>lopsided labia</u> (the fleshy <u>lips</u> around the <u>vagina</u>). If one's big and the other's small, <u>don't worry</u>. You are <u>not</u> deformed.

Not All First Times are the Same

The first time you have sex is usually a bit of a <u>disappointment</u> — especially if you aren't really <u>comfortable</u> about doing it, or if you feel you don't know <u>what</u> you're doing.

Some girls <u>bleed</u> a bit on their first time. This is because a flap of thin skin at the entrance of the vagina gets broken. It can <u>sting</u> a bit when this happens.

This flap of skin — called the <u>hymen</u> — can get broken by itself if a girl does stuff like gymnastics or horse riding or uses <u>tampons</u>. None of these things mean she's not a virgin.

Feeling <u>nervous</u> makes you tense up. If a girl is <u>nervous</u> before sex, her vagina will be tensed up, too. It'll be difficult and painful for her to be penetrated. How <u>relaxed</u> you are depends on how <u>emotionally ready</u> you are for sex.

Oh My — They do ... That?

There's no accounting for taste. People's <u>likes</u> and <u>dislikes</u> in sex are <u>varied</u>. Not <u>everyone</u> likes oral sex. Not <u>everyone</u> likes ham and cheese sarnies, either.

A lot of people are <u>really grossed out</u> by the idea of <u>anal sex</u>. Some people like it, and here's a reason why: men have a gland called the <u>prostate</u>, near the rectum. If they're on the receiving end of anal sex, this gland is stimulated, causing <u>sexual pleasure</u>. Some <u>women</u> enjoy it, too.

Learn about standard-sized bits — same old drill...

Chances are you're <u>completely normal</u>. Not everyone likes the same kind of sex — don't <u>expect</u> everyone to be <u>just like you</u>. There's <u>no reason</u> to feel obliged to do anything that grosses you out.

Myths and Worries about Sex

If you have unprotected sex, then unplanned pregnancy and nasty diseases are the risks you deal with.

It's Not that Difficult to Get Pregnant

For their size, sperm can swim very far, very fast. They have but one aim — to get to the egg and fertilise it. There are hundreds of millions of them in each ejaculation, and it only takes one to get a woman pregnant. The odds are on their side.

The sperm and egg system is pretty effective. Don't think you can cheat it. There's only one 100% effective way to avoid pregnancy, and that's not to have sexual intercourse at all. But assuming that's not for you, then always using condoms is the next best thing.

MYTH: *"You can't get pregnant if you do it standing up."*
TRUTH: Oh yes you can. Sperm can swim upstream and they will.

MYTH: *"You can't get pregnant if you wash yourself out afterwards."*
TRUTH: A sperm can reach the egg in as little as 5 minutes — if you ran, you could get to the shower, but you wouldn't be able to wash all 300 million sperm out of the vagina anyway, so don't try it.

MYTH: *"You can't get pregnant if you do it on your period."*
TRUTH: Sperm can survive inside a girl's body for several days. If she ovulates only 10 days after the start of her period, then there may be live sperm inside her to meet the egg when she ovulates.

MYTH: *"If the boy pulls out before he comes, she won't get pregnant."*
TRUTH: Pulling out doesn't work. There are a few sperm even in the 'pre-cum' that comes out of the boy's penis before he ejaculates.

MYTH: *"If you come outside the vagina, she won't get pregnant."*
TRUTH: Not necessarily. Those little sperm can swim a long way. If he comes at the top of her thigh, the sperm can find their own way into the vagina — especially if there's vaginal wetness there.

MYTH: *"You won't get pregnant on your first time."*
TRUTH: There's no sense to this myth. A girl who has unprotected sex can get pregnant — first time or fiftieth time.

If 100 girls have sex without contraception, about 85 of them will get pregnant.

You Can Catch a Disease from Someone Your Age

A lot more young people than you'd think already have sexually transmitted diseases.

In some parts of the country, one in five women aged 16-20 has chlamydia.

Gonorrhoea is becoming more and more common in younger people. If you have unprotected sex with someone who has it, you've got a 50% chance of catching it. That's a really high chance of infection.

Nearly 40% of people in Britain with AIDS got it when they were in their teens. Very scary.

Put two and two together and get babies...

Bet that scared you. If you have sex, you can't hide away from the risks. Don't rely on chance — I wouldn't call an 85% chance of getting pregnant 'good odds'. It's up to you to make safe choices. Learn the facts. Next time you hear someone spreading ignorance, set them right.

Sex and Relationships

If you've got a boyfriend or girlfriend, then sex is likely to be on the agenda — although for some people it won't be on the agenda until they decide to get married.

Get a Reality Check — for Both of You

You don't have to have sex just because you're going out with someone. There's much more to relationships than sex. Share time together, get to know each other, go and fly a kite or something.

Sex does not equal love

OK, get this straight once and for all. "If you loved me, you'd do it," is a big ugly lie.

Two people who love each other respect each other's feelings. The need to have an orgasm can be fixed by masturbating. The need to wait until you're ready before having sex has to be respected. "If you loved me, you'd wait," makes better sense.

It's best when two people decide to have sex for themselves AND each other. Doing it just for yourself is selfish — doing it just for another person is stupid.

If you expect sex to do miracles for you or your relationship, you'll be very disappointed. Sex has no magic powers.

It isn't how it is in films. Nothing is ever how it is in films (even Star Wars).

Some jedis like to get their light sabre out on the first date.

Talk About Sex Before You Get Naked

If you're too shy to be talking about sex, you shouldn't be doing it yet. Take it slowly. Get comfortable talking about it first, and then do what you're comfortable with.

You need to be able to trust your partner. That's a good idea in any relationship, but it's really important if you're going to have sex. You wouldn't get your kit off in front of just anyone.

Let's bonk!

There is absolutely nothing wrong with deciding not to have sexual intercourse for a while.

Sexual intercourse (penetration) should happen after you've already been involved in some kind of intimate activity. Going straight into intercourse would just feel weird.

sexual golf course...

If you do have sexual intercourse, you'll probably feel different afterwards. Talk to your partner about it. You're a couple, after all.

Just Say It —"If we have sex, we're going to use a condom"

Sort out your contraception/safe sex plan first. It's a great idea to do this together as a couple. Think on this — if a boy's not keen on going to the family planning clinic with his girl, maybe he wouldn't be keen to go to the doctor with her if she did get pregnant.

There's nothing worse than being in a situation where you don't know what to say or do. Talking about contraception needn't be like this. As soon as sex is on the cards, just say "If we have sex, we're going to use condoms," or words to that effect. It's nice and confident.

Let's talk about sex, baby...

Let's face it, you're more likely to have sex if you're in a relationship. If you do want to have sex, say so. If you don't, say so. If all he or she wants is sex, maybe it's time for second thoughts.

Safer Sex

Safer sex is <u>vital</u>. You need to know what's <u>safe</u> and what <u>isn't</u>. This isn't a list of all the sexual activities in the world, just the commonest ones. If you do have sex, make it as <u>safe</u> as you can.

Oral Sex — Can Pass On Diseases

It doesn't matter whether it's a <u>man's bits</u> or a <u>woman's bits</u> getting the oral treatment. You can still pass on diseases. It's wisest to use a condom on a man, and clingfilm on a woman.

The <u>virus</u> that causes <u>AIDS</u> can be passed on through oral sex if you have <u>sores</u> in your mouth.

Vaginal Sex — Only Safe With a Condom

<u>Unprotected</u> vaginal intercourse (sex <u>without</u> a condom) can pass on some <u>nasty diseases</u> — and it can get the girl <u>pregnant</u>.

The <u>virus</u> that causes <u>AIDS</u> can <u>easily</u> be passed from the man's semen to the woman's body — especially if there's not enough <u>lubrication</u> or if the man is a bit rough. <u>Always</u> use <u>condoms</u>.

Anal Sex — Dangerous Without a Condom

You're <u>more likely</u> to catch the <u>virus</u> that causes <u>AIDS</u> through anal sex than vaginal sex. It's easy for the thin skin of the anus to be <u>torn</u> slightly during sex. If you're going to have anal sex, always, always use an <u>extra strength condom</u> and plenty of <u>lubrication</u> (<u>not</u> baby oil, it <u>rots condoms</u>).

Masturbation is Safe in Lots of Ways

Let's face it, <u>almost everyone</u> does it. Just as long as you don't do it in <u>public</u>, or <u>in front</u> of anyone who <u>hasn't said</u> they want to watch, you'll be <u>fine</u>.

1) You don't have to worry about anyone getting <u>pregnant</u>.
2) You don't have to worry if your <u>hand</u> will <u>respect</u> you in the morning.
3) You don't have to have 'that talk' about <u>contraception</u> with your <u>hand</u>.
4) Your <u>hand</u> doesn't care if you <u>fall asleep</u> afterwards.

Masturbation isn't always safe.

It's not dirty, sad or pathetic. It's totally <u>normal</u>, and a <u>great</u> way of exploring your <u>sexuality</u>.

Getting Sexy Without Penetration Is Nice and Safe

It's a <u>safe</u> way of exploring sexual feelings with a partner <u>without</u> having <u>penetrative sex</u>. It can also be <u>foreplay</u> — a warm-up to sexual intercourse.

Remember — sex doesn't have to mean <u>penetration</u>. There are lots of <u>other ways</u> to be sexy, like <u>kissing</u>, sexual <u>touching</u>, talking <u>dirty</u> face to face or on the <u>phone</u>, even sexy <u>emails</u> and <u>text messages</u>.

If you aren't <u>planning</u> to have <u>penetrative sex</u>, be careful you don't get <u>carried away</u> when you're together.

If you're in public, don't do anything that might gross people out.

Safer sex — use your imagination...

The only <u>totally safe</u> sex is <u>no sex at all</u>. Know the <u>risks</u> of each kind of sexual activity. If you do get down and dirty with a partner, make sure you've made it as <u>safe</u> as you possibly can.

Sexually Transmitted Infections

These two pages are about some of the <u>nastier</u> diseases you can get from having <u>unprotected sex</u>.

Check Yourself for Anything Odd

These things are <u>symptoms</u> of a lot of <u>sexually transmitted infections</u> (<u>STI</u>s). If you've got any of them, get yourself checked by a <u>doctor</u>.

1) It <u>hurts to pee</u>. (If you're a girl, this could just be cystitis.)
2) You have a <u>sore</u> or <u>itchy</u> penis or vagina.
3) Women: your <u>vaginal discharge</u> goes <u>yellow</u> or <u>green</u> or starts <u>smelling bad</u>.
4) Men: you have any sort of <u>pus</u> dripping out of the end of your <u>penis</u>.   (Yeeuuich)

Go To the Doctor Or the Clinic

If you think something's wrong with your bits, there are two places to go.

1) Your <u>family doctor</u> will be able to help. If you're under 16, the doctor can <u>only</u> tell your parents if he or she thinks you <u>can't understand</u> the treatment. (More on doctors on P.28.)

2) The Genito-Urinary Medicine (<u>GUM</u>) clinics <u>specialise</u> in dealing with sexually transmitted infections. Whatever you've got, they've seen it all before. The <u>great</u> thing about the GUM clinic is you <u>don't</u> have to give your <u>real name</u> — they <u>won't</u> even tell your <u>doctor</u>.

   If you get <u>treated</u>, make sure your <u>sexual partner</u> gets treated too, or you'll end up with the same thing <u>all over again</u>. The <u>sooner</u> you both get treated, the <u>better</u>.

You Can't Always Tell if You've Got Something

<u>Chlamydia</u> is a <u>common</u> STI that a lot of young people have <u>without even knowing</u>. Most people who have it are aged <u>16-19</u>. If it's left for too long, it messes up a woman's tubes so she <u>can't have children</u>.

<u>Gonorrhoea</u> is a <u>nasty</u> STI. It causes a horrid <u>greenish-yellow</u> gunk in men's penises. Most infected women don't have symptoms, so <u>don't know</u> they're infected. It needs treating with <u>antibiotics</u> from a GP or clinic.

If a woman has <u>genital warts</u> inside her, her partner won't be able to <u>tell</u>. She may <u>not know</u>, either.

It Could Be Something Mild Or It Could Be Serious

Some STIs have really <u>similar</u> symptoms. A thick, itchy, white vaginal discharge <u>usually</u> means thrush, but it <u>could</u> be <u>trichomoniasis</u>, which can eventually cause <u>infertility</u>. It's worth getting things checked out so you <u>know</u> what you're dealing with.

All Sores and Warts need Sorting Out

You can get <u>warts</u> on your <u>penis</u> or around your <u>vagina</u>. (They're not the same as ordinary warts that cause verrucas.) Get them removed at the doctor's or the clinic.

   <u>Crabs</u>, or pubic lice, lay their eggs in your pubic hair. The lice cause some really heavy duty <u>itching</u>. You can get a <u>lotion</u> from the <u>chemist</u> to get rid of crabs.

   <u>Herpes</u> is a kind of genital <u>cold sore</u>. Once you've got it it never goes away, but you can get treatment to stop it coming back as often.

      <u>Syphilis</u> starts with a small <u>painless sore</u> on the penis or vagina. It can get <u>very serious</u> if untreated, so get <u>any sores</u> checked out.

Sexually Transmitted Infections

AIDS — the Big Scary Disease

AIDS is caused by <u>HIV</u> (Human Immunodeficiency Virus). It attacks the cells that help fight disease. AIDS is when the disease has got really <u>serious</u>, and any kind of <u>infection</u>, even the <u>flu</u>, can <u>kill</u>.

1) You can catch it by having <u>vaginal sex</u> or <u>anal sex</u> (and <u>oral sex</u>, if the person's got any <u>sores</u> in their mouth) with someone who's got the HIV virus.

2) You can catch it by <u>sharing needles</u> for <u>injection</u> with someone who's got the HIV virus.

3) In the <u>past</u> it was possible to get it from HIV-contaminated <u>blood transfusions</u> (now ALL blood is checked first so you <u>can't</u> get it this way).

4) <u>Babies</u> can get it direct from their <u>mother's blood</u> when they are in the womb, or after they are born from their <u>mother's milk</u> if the mother is infected.

5) You <u>can't</u> get it from toilet seats, kissing, touching, drinking from the same cup, mosquitos or public swimming pools. <u>Non-penetrative sex</u> is pretty <u>safe</u>.

<u>Anyone</u> can get it, straight, gay or bisexual, by having <u>unprotected</u> sex <u>once</u> with <u>one</u> infected person. A <u>lot</u> of people with HIV caught it when they were <u>teenagers</u>.

Anyone who's <u>shared needles</u> to <u>inject drugs</u> or had <u>unprotected sex</u> is at risk. <u>But</u> so's everyone they've had <u>unprotected sex</u> with, and everyone <u>they've</u> had <u>unprotected sex</u> with, and so on.

There's <u>no cure</u>. People living with the virus take a lot of anti-viral drugs to keep the virus down, but it <u>never</u> goes away. There may be a cure for AIDS in the <u>future</u>, but <u>don't bet on it</u>.

It takes <u>6 months</u> for the virus to show up on tests. It's no good having a test straight after unprotected sex. You have to get tested <u>regularly</u>.

When you have sex, use a <u>condom</u> until you're in a faithful relationship where you know each other's sex histories, and <u>trust</u> each other.

Thrush Doesn't Always Come From Sex

This is something <u>women</u> can <u>just get</u> — it doesn't mean they've caught it through <u>sex</u>.

1) It makes the area around the vagina <u>itch</u> like fury, and the vaginal discharge goes all thick and lumpy like cottage cheese, and it also smells a bit like <u>bread</u>.

2) It's caused by a kind of <u>yeast</u>. If the <u>balance</u> of your insides has been <u>disturbed</u> by taking <u>antibiotics</u>, you can get it. You can also get it if you're <u>diabetic</u>. You can get it from wiping yourself from <u>back</u> to <u>front</u> after you go to the loo.

3) <u>Men</u> can get it too, especially from <u>unprotected sex</u> with a woman who's got it.

If it's the <u>first time</u> you've had it, <u>go to the doc</u> — just to make sure it's only thrush and not anything else. If you've had it before and you know what it is, you can get a cream, or a pill, or pessaries (big pills that you stick up inside you) from the chemist.

Wear <u>cotton undies</u> to keep your bits <u>well aired</u>. Wash them on high heat, or <u>iron</u> the gussets (to <u>kill</u> any <u>yeast</u> that still might be sticking to the pants). <u>Avoid</u> wearing <u>tights</u> while you've got thrush.

Fancy eating spotted dick — thought not...

EEEEEEWWW! It's in <u>your interest</u> to know the <u>symptoms</u> that mean you should go straight to the doc. Think about why you should <u>use condoms</u> and get <u>tested regularly</u> if you're sexually active.

Protected Sex

Unless you're <u>exclusively gay</u>, you need to think about the possibility of <u>getting pregnant</u>, or getting somebody else pregnant. Everyone, gay or straight needs to think about <u>avoiding STIs</u>.

Getting Pregnant Shouldn't be a Surprise

That's <u>why</u> people use <u>contraception</u>. Remember, if you're <u>embarrassed</u> to carry condoms around with you, you'll be <u>more</u> embarrassed carrying a <u>big pregnant belly</u> around, or <u>pushing a pram</u>.

Think about contraception <u>before</u> you decide to have sex.
If you have sex, talk about contraception <u>before</u> you get naked.

It's Men's responsibility and Women's too

Lads — <u>offer</u> to <u>use a condom</u> for sex. Don't wait till your partner asks you.
Don't <u>assume</u> a girl's on the <u>pill</u>.
Of course, <u>you</u> can't get pregnant, but you <u>can</u> get an <u>STI</u>.

Lasses — if he <u>doesn't</u> offer to use a condom then go ahead and <u>ask him</u>.
If he tries to <u>talk</u> you <u>out</u> of using a condom, he's not <u>emotionally mature</u> enough for sex.
Obviously, <u>he</u> can't get <u>pregnant</u>, so there's <u>less at stake</u> for him.

Condoms are Great for Contraception and Safe Sex

Just to make absolutely sure you know, a condom is a sort of <u>latex sheath</u> — it's worn <u>over the penis</u> during intercourse and <u>collects</u> the ejaculated semen.

They're <u>99% effective</u> if they're used <u>properly</u>.

You can get <u>free condoms</u> from any <u>family planning clinic</u> (find the nearest one in the Yellow Pages) You can buy them in <u>chemists</u>, <u>supermarkets</u>, <u>vending machines</u> and <u>garages</u> — unlike other kinds of contraception.

3 Condoms
for safe sex

How to Put On a Condom

Nope, this isn't like a class — no bananas or courgettes here, just the facts.

1) Condoms only go onto an <u>erect</u> penis. If there's a <u>rip</u> or <u>tear</u> in the condom, then it <u>isn't</u> safe to use. Be careful not to <u>snag</u> the condom on your <u>fingernails</u>.

2) Don't unroll it first, just put it over the <u>tip</u> of the penis with the ring on the outside.

3) Grab the <u>teat</u> on the end and hold it tight so <u>no air</u> gets trapped inside.
<u>Keep hold</u> of it above the tip of the penis while putting the condom on.

I lied. There is a banana.

4) <u>Roll</u> the condom down the penis right to the base.

5) After sex, <u>withdraw</u> quickly and <u>remove</u> the condom carefully.

6) Throw it away somewhere sensible — in the bin, <u>not</u> down the toilet.
<u>Never</u> reuse a condom.

7) Use condoms for <u>whatever</u> you're doing. There are <u>flavoured</u> ones for <u>oral sex</u> and specially <u>thick</u> ones for <u>anal sex</u>.

Careful — <u>baby oil</u> and <u>vaseline</u> eat <u>holes</u> in condoms. Yikes.

A Femidom is like a Condom for Women

It's like a <u>mini bin-liner</u> with rubber rings at both ends. The top ring at the closed end goes right up inside the vagina, and the bottom ring <u>sticks out</u> outside the vagina. Some women <u>like</u> them, some <u>hate</u> them.

Protected Sex

All the contraception on this page does <u>nothing at all</u> to protect against <u>STIs</u>.

The Pill stops Pregnancy Happening

The <u>contraceptive pill</u> works by changing the <u>hormones</u> in a woman's body that get her ready for an egg to be fertilised. There are two types of pill — <u>combined</u> and <u>progesterone only</u>.

It's over 99% effective in preventing pregnancy if it's used properly.
You have to remember to take the pill <u>every day</u>, not just when you have sex.

pill

COMBINED PILL	
How it works	It <u>stops ovulation</u> from happening. It also makes it <u>harder</u> for an egg to be <u>fertilised</u> or to <u>implant</u> in the womb.
What to do if you miss one	If it's <u>less</u> than <u>12 hours</u> since you should have taken it, <u>take it now</u>. If it's <u>more</u> than 12 hours, take the <u>next</u> one at the right time, and use <u>condoms</u> for <u>7 days</u>. <u>Always</u> check the instructions in your pack of pills.

PROGESTERONE ONLY (MINI-PILL)	
How it works	It makes it harder for an egg to be <u>fertilised</u> or to <u>implant</u> in the womb.
What to do if you miss one	If it's <u>less</u> than <u>3 hours</u> since you should have taken it, take it now. If it's more than <u>3 hours</u>, take the <u>next</u> one at the right time, and use <u>condoms</u> for <u>2 days</u>. <u>Always</u> check the instructions in your pack of pills.

The pill has some <u>side effects</u>, like <u>feeling sick</u> and <u>putting on weight</u>.
Not every woman gets these side effects. Different brands of each type of pill have different side effects — the <u>doctor</u> or the <u>family planning clinic</u> will explain them.

There are <u>other reasons</u> for taking the pill besides <u>contraception</u>.
1) It can make periods <u>lighter</u>, which can help with <u>bad period pain</u>.
2) Some brands of the pill can help with <u>skin problems</u>, like <u>acne</u>.

> Men can go with their girlfriends to get the pill.

Other Contraception for Women (in stable relationships)

1) DEPO-PROVERA is an <u>injection</u> that you have every three months. It's good if you are in a stable, faithful relationship but have trouble <u>remembering</u> to take the <u>pill</u>. It's over 99% effective.

2) The DIAPHRAGM or CAP is a little <u>rubber bowl</u> that fits over the cervix (right up inside the vagina). It's a bit fiddly, and it has to be fitted by a nurse the first time. You have to use messy <u>spermicide</u> gel or cream with it.

3) The IUD, or COIL is a <u>T-shaped</u> plastic and wire <u>thingy</u> that goes right up <u>inside the womb</u> (uterus). It can make periods heavier and more painful. It's fitted by a nurse.

The Morning After Pill isn't a contraceptive — it's a Last Resort

The 'Morning After' pill is a <u>heavy dose</u> of the <u>same hormones</u> that are in the contraceptive pill. If it's taken up to <u>72 hours</u> after unprotected sex, it prevents a fertilised egg from implanting in the womb. You can get it from the <u>doctor</u>, the <u>family planning clinic</u>, or some <u>chemists</u>.

It's all about levels of protection...

Remember, only <u>condoms</u>, <u>femidoms</u>, or <u>not having sex</u> protect you against STIs <u>and</u> pregnancy.
You need to be in a secure faithful relationship <u>before</u> you rely on other kinds of contraception.

Being Attractive

<u>Most</u> people are pretty concerned about whether they're <u>attractive</u> or not — and whether they'll ever manage to pull. Curiously, people seem to pay loads of attention to their own physical <u>appearance</u> but hardly any to the <u>way they behave</u>.

<u>Attractiveness</u> comes in Lots of Different Ways

The thing to remember is that you can't change the shape of your body overnight, but you can make sure you have things like <u>clean hair</u> and a <u>nice smile</u>.

Think about all the 'gorgeous' people on <u>telly</u>. They've all got <u>personal stylists</u> and <u>hairdressers</u> to make the most of their looks.

If you saw them with <u>dirty hair</u>, <u>no make up</u> and a <u>gormless expression</u> on their face, they wouldn't look half so pretty.

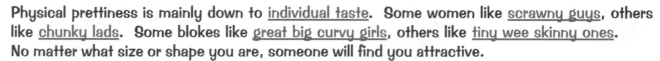

Also, sometimes people think that celebrities are attractive <u>just because</u> they're <u>famous</u>. Odd.

It's not just <u>girls</u> who worry about their bodies.
Boys worry that they're not <u>hunky</u> enough.

There's a lot more to masculinity than muscles. Most lasses find a <u>nice personality</u> more important than a <u>six-pack</u> tummy.

Physical prettiness is mainly down to <u>individual taste</u>. Some women like <u>scrawny guys</u>, others like <u>chunky lads</u>. Some blokes like <u>great big curvy girls</u>, others like <u>tiny wee skinny ones</u>. No matter what size or shape you are, someone will find you attractive.

Good Looks Don't make you Happy — just Look Around

1) It's <u>easy</u> to think that the <u>beautiful people</u> will have the <u>nicest lives</u>. In fact, everyone's life has a fair share of good bits and bad bits. Good looks aren't a free ticket to happiness.

2) <u>Personality</u> is definitely the most <u>important</u> part of falling for somebody — you can easily be <u>attracted</u> to someone <u>without</u> actually thinking they're <u>really good looking</u>.

Fantastic! You've got a spot too.

Everyone's got <u>different tastes</u>. Some people like quiet types, others go for people who are always larking about. There's no perfect personality, just like there's no perfect body. The key is to <u>be yourself</u>.

3) One thing's for sure — it pays to make the <u>most</u> of what you've <u>got</u>. That means doing things that your <u>mum</u> would nag you to do — <u>brush</u> your <u>hair</u>, clean your <u>teeth</u>, tuck that <u>shirt</u> in...

Even if you're cultivating a <u>mean and moody</u> image, a <u>smile</u> wins hearts like nothing else.

Be <u>confident</u> when you talk to people, but don't get over-cocky. It's not attractive to come across as fake or arrogant.

4) Here's some <u>bad news</u> — you'll almost certainly get a <u>huge spot</u> just before a date. It's a law of nature and there's not much you can do about it. On the bright side — if both of you have got an enormous spot, it'll give you something to <u>talk about</u>.

The look of love...

Everyone <u>worries</u> about being fanciable. The way forward is to be <u>yourself</u> and be <u>confident</u>. Don't forget to wash and scrub up — it'll go farther than you think to <u>help you pull</u> your dream boy or girl.

Pregnancy

Not many people plan on having kids when they're still at school — but you'd be surprised how often it happens. Read on — it's important.

Think About Pregnancy Before You Have Sex

Every year there are about 90,000 teenage pregnancies in Britain — and 8,000 to girls under 16. That's a heck of a lot of unsafe sex going on.

Pregnancy can be fab. Most people end up having kids some day, but when you're at school isn't really the best time, let's face it. And don't think "it won't happen to me" — most teen pregnancies are accidents.

Missing a Period Could Mean You're Pregnant

1) Most women realise they might be pregnant when their period doesn't arrive.

2) If that happens, don't panic. You can buy pregnancy tester kits from chemists. They check for chemicals in your pee, and change colour if you are pregnant. Most kits come in packs of 2, so do both tests to be sure of the result. If you get different results, you'd best see a doctor.

3) Some people are too scared or embarrassed to buy a kit. They'll need to see a doctor or go to a family planning clinic sharpish. It's hard but really important.

4) If you're a bloke, you might be thinking 'What do I care?' Well if it's your girlfriend, pal, you'd better think again. If she's worried about it then buy her a test pack — it's a lot less awkward than finding out you're going to be a daddy from the gossip round school.

5) You might NOT be pregnant — there are other reasons for a period to be late. But it's best to check, believe me. If you are, you will need to see a doctor at some point.

Hey babe, I got you the kit.

The Sooner You Get Help the Better

If you have unprotected sex, or something goes wrong, like a condom splitting, then don't wait around for your period — head to a clinic or a doctor pronto. If you're quick enough they can give you the morning-after pill (see P.13). And if you're a bloke, don't just leave it up to her — give her some support or go with her.

Pregnancy Isn't Just a Girl Thing

Just because the bloke doesn't actually get pregnant, that doesn't mean he's got no responsibilities. At the end of the day he got his jollies too, so he'll have to deal with the consequences as well.

If the girl decides to have the child, the father's got to make his mind up about whether to support her or not — helping to look after the child, giving her emotional support and all that. He can't just walk away — it's his baby too.

Sex, sex, sex — got your attention yet...

Crikey — it's all pretty scary stuff. Just remember, getting pregnant isn't the end of the world, but it's worth thinking about before you embark on a life of rampant sex. And it isn't just a girl thing.

16

Your Choices

If you do end up pregnant you'll have to make some really tough decisions. There's no point in trying to hide from it — you won't find any easy answers here, just the facts.

Being Pregnant Can Be Really Tough

A woman's body goes through a lot in pregnancy. She gets bigger and bigger, she may puke a lot, she gets upset more easily, she can find it hard to move about. She can even feel the baby kicking inside her.

She's tired so she can't go out much, and she has to give up drinking and smoking in case she harms the baby. Her lifestyle has to change while she carries this enormous weight around inside her for 9 whole months — and all because some lad had sex with her. Then she's got to give birth. It's not easy.

Blokes, you can't just expect the girl to do what you want — she's the one who has to carry the kid around inside her. But you need to know what the options are too.

The baby's dad only has parental rights in law if: 1) He's married to the baby's mum,   OR...
2) She's agreed to give him parental rights,   OR... 3) He's got a court order giving him parental rights.

If You're Pregnant You've Got Three Choices

HAVING THE BABY : You can choose to have the baby and bring it up yourself. That's gonna mean telling your family and friends and the lad involved, if you haven't already. It means making a decision that you're ready enough to have a child and prepared to make sacrifices to do it.

ABORTION : You can choose to have an abortion up to 24 weeks into the pregnancy. You can arrange one on the NHS and no one ever need know about it. But there are loads of reasons why you might not want one — especially if your family has a moral objection. It's not an easy way out — see P.17.

ADOPTION : The other option is to have the baby and give it up for adoption. It'll go to people who really want a baby but maybe can't have one. They'll be able to afford to give it a nice life. Unfortunately, you'll have to go through the whole pregnancy, and give birth to the child and then give it up — it can be really devastating.

Think about the Consequences of What You Do

1) You don't have to tell everyone — but you need to talk things through with someone who won't flip their lid and won't blab to anyone else. OK, it's you who's going to have this thing inside you, but there are other people who may want to get involved — like the bloke or your parents.

2) If you want to have the baby, you'll definitely have to tell your parents. There'll be loads of practical stuff to sort out — like whether you're going to live at home with them, and how you're going to finish school.

The longer Keri kept her secret, the bigger the hat she needed to keep it under.

3) If you go for adoption, remember the bloke involved or your family may put pressure on you to keep it.

4) Be ready for people's reactions — you don't know how they'll take the news. And if you keep it secret, remember that they may eventually find out and be angry you didn't tell them. Even your parents and friends may be negative or criticise you — so you'll need to be strong whatever you decide to do.

Consequences — they come to all of us...

There may be options, but none of them are exactly easy. The bottom line is you've got to decide — not just what to do, but who to tell. Talking to someone could really help you work out what to do.

Section Three — Having Kids

Abortion

Any discussions about <u>abortion</u> can be heated, and sometimes the <u>facts</u> get <u>lost</u>, so here they are.

These are the Facts about Abortion

1) Abortion is legal in <u>England</u>, <u>Scotland</u> and <u>Wales</u> up to the <u>24th week</u> of pregnancy. Abortions are only allowed after that time if the pregnancy would probably <u>kill</u> the woman or if there is something <u>very seriously wrong</u> with the foetus.

2) <u>Most</u> abortions are carried out <u>before the 12th week</u> of pregnancy.

3) A woman needs to get the <u>agreement</u> of <u>two doctors</u> before she can have an abortion. The doctors need to agree that the woman's <u>physical</u> or <u>mental health</u> would <u>suffer badly</u> if she didn't have an abortion.

4) A legal abortion is <u>very safe</u> for the woman. She <u>can</u> have children later in life if she wants.

5) A <u>man</u> doesn't have the legal right to <u>stop</u> his girlfriend or wife from having an abortion.

<u>Age of foetus</u>	<u>Type of abortion</u>
Less than 9 weeks	"Abortion Pill" — starts contractions which feel like very bad period pain, pregnancy ends like a miscarriage.
9-12 weeks	Vacuum suction — contents of the womb are sucked out.
13-19 weeks	Dilation of the cervix and removal of the contents of the womb by forceps and suction — this time under anaesthetic.
20-24 weeks	Dilation of the cervix and suction removal of the contents of the womb. This is done in two stages.

<u>No</u> type of contraception is <u>100% effective</u> even if it's <u>used properly</u>. If you have vaginal sexual intercourse, there is <u>always</u> a risk of <u>unplanned pregnancy</u>.

See Your Doctor — or the Family Planning Clinic

If your doctor doesn't agree to an abortion, you can see <u>a different doctor</u>. Getting the agreement of two doctors isn't hard — the first doctor will refer you to a second doctor, often at the <u>hospital</u> or the <u>abortion clinic</u>.

The <u>Family Planning Clinic</u> is a good place to go if you don't want to see your family doctor. The nearest one will be in the phone book.

The <u>British Pregnancy Advisory Service</u> and <u>Marie Stopes</u> are private organisations that give contraception and abortion services. You have to <u>pay</u> for your treatment from them.

There'll be Ups and Downs to your Decisions

Whether a girl decides to have an <u>abortion</u>, have the baby <u>adopted</u> or <u>keep the baby</u>, she may well feel kind of <u>down</u> and <u>weepy</u> for a while afterwards. Even if she made the best decision for her, there are still <u>downsides</u> to everything. There are <u>no easy choices</u>, and no real right answers.

You make your own choices...

Remember, contraception is <u>not 100% effective</u>. An <u>unplanned pregnancy</u> is something you might have to consider one day. It helps to know all the facts about the different options beforehand.

Bringing Up a Child

Being a parent <u>isn't</u> about looking after a lovey-dovey doll — it's about dealing with this screaming, snotty, messy ankle-biter that <u>can't do anything</u> for itself. Then there's the <u>practical</u> stuff...

Parenthood's a <u>Job for Life</u>

Children <u>can't look after</u> themselves — they need feeding, clothing and washing. They also need to be well-treated, healthy and educated — and that's down to the <u>parents</u> from <u>babyhood to 18</u>.

Things are Gonna <u>Change</u> Forever

Like, duh! I know this is <u>mindnumbingly obvious</u>, but it still needs saying again. Being a parent is hard work — look at the facts, and if you don't like 'em, <u>use a condom</u> or <u>don't have sex</u>. Simple.

Harsh Reality Stores

Open

Exciting offer
Nappies:
2 packs for £10

1) **WHERE YOU ARE GOING TO LIVE:**

- If someone has a baby while they're living <u>at home</u>, their own parents may <u>not</u> be too thrilled about it.
- New mums often have to find <u>their own place</u> — which costs <u>money</u>.

Carefree Corner

Movie Offer
2 go for £10

CD £10

Pizza
2 for £10

Happy...
...music

2) **WHERE THE MONEY WILL COME FROM:**

- Parents get government <u>help</u>, but if they're <u>not earning money</u> things can get tight.
- The father of the child can <u>do his bit</u>, but if he's still at school, he can't do <u>much</u>.
- The money you'd spend on <u>clothes</u>, <u>music</u> or <u>going out</u> goes on the baby instead.

3) **WHAT COULD HAPPEN TO YOUR RELATIONSHIPS:**

- People's <u>attitudes</u> to new parents change.
- <u>Relatives</u> will have an <u>opinion</u> on everything you do with the child.
- It's harder to see <u>friends</u> too — their lives are going on <u>without you</u>.

4) **WHAT WILL CHANGE IN YOUR LIFESTYLE:**

- The big one is <u>school</u> — if you're still in education then you'll have to <u>leave</u> for a bit. That may mean you won't have any qualifications for a while. There's no reason why you can't <u>go back</u> to your education later on, though.
- Parents <u>can't go out</u> when they want without arranging babysitters.
- If the mum's breastfeeding, then she <u>can't drink</u> much, and <u>smoking</u> around little kids can do them <u>serious damage</u>. The child may <u>not sleep well</u>, so no one else in the house'll get much sleep either.

Don't Forget — the Child's a Person Too

It's <u>not</u> just about what <u>you want</u> any more. Right from day one, the child is a <u>person</u>, with <u>thoughts</u> and <u>emotions</u> of its own. So the kid's dependent on you, but it has its own <u>rights</u> too.

A baby's for life not just for christening...

It all looks so terrifying — but remember, it's the same for <u>all new parents</u>, whatever age they are. Life doesn't <u>suddenly end</u> when people have children — but it's worth <u>waiting</u> until you feel ready.

Choosing to Become Parents

I can't help wondering <u>why</u> people have sprogs — it seems like such an <u>odd thing</u> to do, given all the <u>hassle</u> it can cause. Or maybe I just like sleep too much.

There are Good and Bad Reasons for Having Kids

Not every child is an accident. Like I said before, <u>most people</u> end up having kids sooner or later. And some of them <u>choose</u> to.

But darling, you can't leave. It'll break Tristan's heart.

1) A lot of people <u>try to wait</u> until they feel <u>ready</u> to have kids. For some people being "ready" means being <u>married</u>, or having enough <u>money</u>, or just getting that <u>weird urge</u> to have a child.

2) Of course, having kids <u>isn't</u> that simple — some people have <u>problems</u> conceiving. They can decide to have <u>fertility treatment</u> to have a baby, or they can <u>adopt</u> — taking a child into their family by law.

3) Some people have kids because they think it'll be <u>someone to love them</u> — maybe because their partners or families treat them <u>badly</u>. Unfortunately, it often means they don't think about the <u>practical side</u> of having a child, or exactly how much <u>work</u> is involved.

4) Other people have kids to try to <u>save a relationship</u>. They think that if their partner wants to <u>leave them</u>, then having a child will make them <u>want to stay</u>. Problem is, it usually makes things <u>worse</u> — the partner might be unhappy, and it may be better all round if the relationship ended.

Bringing Up Kids is Easier if There are Two of You

Bringing up kids is easier if there are two people in a <u>stable relationship</u> to share the hassle and stress. That's not to say <u>single parents</u> can't do it — but they'll have twice the work to do.

Here're some things about <u>marriage</u> for you to chew over in your mind.

Four Great Reasons to Get Married

- A good marriage gives a <u>stable relationship</u> for bringing up children.
- The marriage means the two parents are bound together <u>in law</u>, which gives <u>security</u>. Obviously a <u>bad</u> marriage <u>doesn't</u> give security.
- A <u>happy couple</u> work together as a <u>team</u>, making everything easier and nicer than battling on alone (which is actually true of <u>all</u> good stable relationships, not just marriages).
- There are loads of <u>tax benefits</u> for married couples with nippers.

Come on Dad FASTER... and then later can we go to the Zoo again... please Dad, pleeeeease.....

Thing is, <u>just</u> having kids is <u>no reason</u> to get married. It's better for people to get married because they <u>want to</u>, or feel <u>ready to</u> — and then think about kids. Otherwise things could go wrong — and a <u>divorce</u> is <u>horrible</u> for children to go through.

But frankly <u>anyone</u> who wants to be a parent deserves loads of <u>respect</u> in my book.

Want to get married — give us a ring...

People want kids — it's a fact of life... well, it's <u>THE fact of life</u> I s'pose. This page is all about <u>why</u> people want kids, and <u>when</u> it'd be better or worse to have them. Could be <u>handy</u> to know one day.

Revision Summary

Whether or not you've started having sex, and whether or not you ever want to have kids — you need to know the facts about sex and having kids. These questions test if you know your stuff — and if you know how to deal with a few sticky situations.

Questions on Section Two — Sex

1) How old do you have to be to have sex legally?

2) If a 17 year old boy has sex with his 24 year old female English teacher, could either of them get into trouble with the law?

3) If you've taken someone out on a date, and spoiled them rotten, should they give you sex out of politeness? Do you have the right to demand sex? Give reasons for your answers.

4) If a girl isn't having sex with boys is she necessarily ugly, frigid or lesbian?

5) Is having sex a good way to boost your self-respect? Give a reason for your answer.

6) Is it normal for a boy to have one testicle bigger than the other?

7) Will every girl bleed the first time she has sex?

8) Can a girl get pregnant if: a) it's her first time?   b) the boy pulls out before he comes?
c) she washes herself out afterwards?

9) What percentage of current AIDS sufferers in Britain caught it while they were teenagers?

10) If you and your boyfriend/girlfriend decide to have sex, when should you talk about contraception?

11) Why should you use a condom if you have vaginal sex?

12) If you've had unprotected sex, and you get itchy and sore afterwards, what should you do?

13) Name two ways in which HIV can be transmitted.

14) Where can you get free condoms?

15) How should you put on a condom?

16) If a girl is on the combined contraceptive pill, and forgets to take one, what should she do?

Questions on Section Three — Having Kids

1) If you're a girl, what should you do if you miss a period? Why?
If you're a bloke, what should you do if your girlfriend misses a period? Why?

2) Do you think it's better to find out one way or the other, or leave it as long as you can? Why?

3) Where can you buy pregnancy tester kits?

4) Where can you go for a pregnancy test if you don't want to buy a tester kit?

5) Name 5 things that happen to a woman during pregnancy.

6) What are the three choices a girl has if she is pregnant?

7) Why do you think it's important to think about the consequences of each choice?

8) When someone has a baby, how does their life change?

9) Why do you think people have kids?

10) Give three reasons why it can be easier to bring up kids in a marriage.

Racism

Racism can be caused by loads of things, like ignorance or fear of anybody who isn't the same. It is a real problem and it's not something you can just shrug off.

There are Loads of Ethnic Backgrounds in the UK

Britain's made up of all sorts of different ethnic backgrounds — different cultures we or our ancestors came from.
For example, some Jewish people came from Europe in the 1930s to escape the Nazis. And many people from India, Pakistan, Bangladesh, Ireland and the Caribbean came to find work in the 1940s and the 1950s.

Even so-called Anglo-Saxons are a mix of Celtic, Saxon (German), Jute (Danish) and Norman (French).

There are people from all over the place. It's something that makes Britain a cool place to be.

Racism is Thinking You're Better than Other Races

Racial prejudice is when a person treats someone as an inferior because they have a different skin colour, culture, religion or nationality. It can be blatant — physically attacking people and giving them verbal abuse, or turning people down for jobs, all of which is illegal. It can also be more subtle, but still pretty nasty — like making someone feel unwelcome in a pub or shop, or giving them the cold shoulder when they're new in the area, all because they're from a different ethnic background.

Take Stereotypes with a Pinch of Salt

Some people assume everyone from an ethnic group is the same. They don't think of them as individuals — they just think in terms of stereotypes. You'll hear rubbish like, "They're all lazy," or "They're terrorists," or "They've come to steal our jobs." Gullible people hear that sort of thing and start believing it. But can you think of two people you know who are exactly the same as each other? You can't. It's awesome just how different everybody is — you can only make your mind up about people one by one.

You wouldn't want someone to turn against you because they didn't like a couple of the kids in your street. Well it's just as stupid to treat somebody in a certain way because of their ethnic background.

Racist Insults Aren't Funny or Clever

There are always some people who think it's smart to insult people or take the mickey out of them because of their skin colour or the culture they come from — you've probably come across it yourself or with someone you know.

1) If everyone just goes along with behaviour like that and acts like it's OK then it starts to seem OK.
2) The next thing is it doesn't seem as bad to attack and hurt people for racist reasons.
3) If you hear someone making racist comments, even as a 'joke', the best thing you can do is tell them what you think about it.
4) If you're the butt of a 'joke' don't put up with it. If it's not going to put you in danger tell the person exactly why what they're saying is narrow-minded and stupid.
5) You can always get the police involved if somebody's giving you a lot of racially-motivated grief.

There's No Such Thing as 'Race' Anyway

Really, there isn't, scientifically speaking. There's as much genetic variation between two random white people as there is between one random white person and one random black person. Skin colour is no more genetically important than all the other differences, it's just more obvious.

Britain's just like the Olympics — loads of different races...

This isn't just a matter of black and white — it's about how you treat other people, whatever their background or skin colour. After all, life would be dead boring if we were all exactly the same.

People With Disabilities

Disability is one of those things some people like to ignore. But sometimes it's worse than that.
People with disabilities can lose out on jobs and a lot of other chances in life because of prejudice.

Disabilities sometimes make people feel awkward

Some people find it difficult to be around the disabled. They try to avoid talking
or even looking at them — almost as if they're afraid of catching something.

Other people stop and stare — as if they're watching some sort of freak show.

It's usually not meant as a deliberate sort of prejudice — it comes from people
feeling awkward at seeing something different from what they call "normal".

But just because someone speaks in a funny way, or can't see, or
uses a wheelchair doesn't make them any less of a human being.

Physical Disability Doesn't Mean Mental Disability

One common myth is that a physically disabled person must be mentally disabled too.
It's an easy excuse for ignoring the person in conversations or treating them like a child.

Think about it — how do you like being treated like a child...
That's how a lot of disabled people feel all the time — really patronised.

People with cerebral palsy have a lot of trouble controlling their muscles and find it hard to speak clearly. Their brains work just as well as yours or mine.	Deaf people often speak with odd voices, because they can't hear the sounds they make. Again, it's got nothing to do with intelligence at all.

And anyway there are lots of different kinds of mental disability, going from being a bit slow
to being pretty much unable to lead an adult life. You can't just make simple judgements.

> Disabled people have a right to a fun life — same as everyone else.

Treat Disabled People the Same as Anyone Else

A disabled person is just as likely to be clever, thick, funny, boring, sarcastic,
horny or annoying as anyone else.

There's no need to be afraid of talking to disabled people for fear of doing or
saying the wrong thing — just treat them the same as anyone else.

Talk directly to them, not to the people with them. Don't talk to them
as if they were children — just talk normally. If they have a problem
hearing or understanding you, then they'll let you know.

Be patient if you're talking to someone with a speech problem —
it's just as frustrating for them if you can't understand what they're saying.

Being able-bodied — it doesn't make you that special...

Disability prejudice isn't usually deliberate — most of the time it comes from people not thinking.
The thing is, all you have to do is think carefully about how you'd like to be treated and just do that!

Gender Prejudice

Here's yet another topic that tends to start <u>heated debates</u> in the classroom.

Men <u>and</u> Women <u>are</u> People

Unbelievably <u>obvious</u>, but worth saying. <u>Everyone</u> deserves <u>respect</u> because they're a <u>human being</u>. Men don't get <u>extra</u> respect for being <u>men</u>, and women don't get <u>extra</u> for being <u>women</u>.

Unfortunately, things aren't quite that simple or easy to sort out...

Not <u>All</u> Men/Women are Like <u>That</u>!

People make lots of <u>generalisations</u> about men and women, like "men are better drivers" and "women are more sympathetic". They <u>aren't</u> all true. They <u>definitely</u> aren't true for <u>every</u> last man and <u>every</u> last woman.

Will Work for Food.
(No Wimmen's Jobs.)

If you <u>don't fit</u> into a generalisation, it doesn't mean there's something <u>wrong</u> with you. A girl who is <u>outgoing</u>, <u>logical</u> and <u>tough</u> is still female. A boy who is <u>quiet</u>, <u>emotional</u> and <u>caring</u> is still male.

It's the same with <u>jobs</u>. Some people have <u>old-fashioned ideas</u> about how women don't make good managers, or men shouldn't be nurses and so on.

But really people should choose jobs based on what they <u>want to do</u> and what they're <u>good at</u> — <u>not</u> what sex they are.

Sex Discrimination <u>is</u> Unfair Treatment

Sex discrimination is <u>treating people unfairly</u> because of their gender. It's OK for some things to be different for men and women though — like public loos and changing rooms for a start.

There is Less Discrimination Nowadays

Nowadays there's a lot <u>less</u> discrimination than there used to be — and there are <u>laws</u> against it. Women <u>and</u> men can do <u>almost any</u> job they want to — whether it's being a nurse or being Prime Minister. But there are still <u>some differences</u> in the way men and women are treated.

- Women don't always get paid as much as men for doing the same work.
- Very few women become top managers — but attitudes are changing.
- Women aren't allowed to fight as front-line soldiers.

- Men don't get paid paternity leave when their baby is born — but women get paid leave.
- Men almost never get custody of children in a divorce settlement — the mother does.
- Many people look down on men who are victims of violence or abuse by women.

Equality of the sexes — how do you put it into practice...

Equal rights is a tough one alright — I mean it makes <u>perfect sense</u> that everyone should be treated <u>fairly</u> and <u>equally</u>. But it doesn't always work in practice — there's a lot <u>less discrimination</u> nowadays, but there's still <u>some</u>. It's all about <u>attitudes</u> — and they can take time to change.

Sexuality and Sexual Orientation

This is a topic that really makes people <u>nervous</u> — in fact some people are downright <u>scared</u> of it. Thing is, you can't just brush it under the carpet. Sooner or later you <u>will</u> have to deal with it.

No One Chooses to be Gay

Let's get a few of the <u>myths</u> cleared up first.

Being <u>gay</u> means being <u>sexually attracted</u> almost always to people of the <u>same sex</u> as you. Being <u>straight</u> means being <u>sexually attracted</u> almost always to people of the <u>opposite sex</u> to you. Being <u>sexually attracted</u> to people of <u>both sexes</u> is called <u>bisexuality</u>.

> <u>Gay</u> people <u>do not choose</u> to be gay. They just are.
>
> <u>Straight</u> people <u>do not choose</u> to be straight. They just are.
>
> <u>Bisexual</u> people <u>do not choose</u> to be bi. They just are. (They're <u>not</u> 'undecided' either.)

Homosexual Does Not mean Paedophile

A homosexual fancies people of <u>their own sex</u>. Homosexual sex is <u>legal</u> for consenting adults.

A paedophile is someone, straight or gay, who fancies <u>children</u>. Sex with children is <u>illegal</u>. (See P.4)

You Can't Treat People Differently for Being Gay

Be clear about this — <u>teasing</u> or <u>physically attacking</u> people because of their sexuality is <u>wrong</u>. In fact, it's <u>against the law</u> to discriminate against people of different sexualities.

> Some people think that <u>being gay</u> isn't wrong, but actually <u>having sex</u> with people of the <u>same sex</u> is a <u>sin</u>. On the other hand, some people think it's <u>unfair</u> that <u>straight</u> people are able to <u>act</u> on their <u>sexual feelings</u>, but not <u>gay</u> people.

But whatever your <u>opinions</u> are — they <u>shouldn't</u> affect the way you treat people.

Not All Gays or Lesbians are the Same

Some people have a definite <u>picture</u> in their head about <u>gay men</u> and <u>women</u> — often <u>without</u> really knowing <u>anyone</u> who <u>fits</u> the picture.

It's one of the things that leads to <u>stereotypes</u> — and to <u>prejudice</u>.

Some people think <u>lesbians</u> are all <u>butch</u> women with <u>short hair</u>, <u>dungarees</u> and <u>sensible shoes</u>. Not true.

I thought we were supposed to wear sensible shoes...

Some people think <u>gay men</u> all flap their hands a lot and talk with a lisp. That's called being <u>camp</u>, and although <u>some</u> gay men are <u>very camp</u>, not all are. Some <u>straight</u> men are <u>camp</u>, too.

Discussing sexuality — are you comfortable yet...

Blimey, it's a tricky area this — a lot of people have <u>strong opinions</u> about it. But that shouldn't affect how you <u>treat</u> gay people. They <u>aren't</u> all stereotypes — and they are <u>not</u> paedophiles.

Revision Summary for Prejudice

This section doesn't cover everything to do with prejudice. In fact, it only scratches the surface of the issues here. But that doesn't mean you can just skip over it — no way. These are four of the biggest issues you'll come across in life. And sadly, this section's about how people take the stupidest things and use them as an excuse to treat other people badly — by teasing, insulting or even attacking them. These questions are here to get you thinking a bit — after all, these things affect you too...

1) Give two examples of racist behaviour.

2) Think of an example of a sterotype about people from an ethnic group. Is it true for all the people from that ethnic group?

3) Do you have to be white to be a racist? Explain your answer.

4) What does it mean to be British in your opinion?

5) Most 'Anglo-Saxons' are a mix of ethnic backgrounds. Name two of them.

6) How is it scientifically possible to say there's no such thing as race?

7) Why might some people feel awkward around a disabled person? Give one reason.

8) Give two examples of prejudice against disabled people.

9) What effect does cerebral palsy have on people's bodies?
    What effect does it have on their brains?

10) Name two ways you could treat disabled people the same as anyone else.

11) Give two examples of generalisations people make about men and women.

12) Some people have old-fashioned ideas about the jobs men and women can do.
    Give two examples.

13) What is sex discrimination?

14) There are still some differences in the way men and women are treated nowadays.
    Give three examples.

15) What does "being gay" mean?

16) What does "being straight" mean?

17) What does "being bisexual" mean?

18) Explain the difference between homosexuals and paedophiles.

19) People have lots of different opinions about sexuality. Give two examples of
    commonly held beliefs.

Getting Hot and Sweaty

Doing exercise is like <u>wearing deodorant</u>. It's something <u>everyone</u> ought to do.
You don't have to be <u>Olympic standard</u> though — just make a bit of an <u>effort</u>.

Exercise *Isn't Only* for *Sporty Types*

Everyone needs to do exercise. It doesn't have to leave you flat out to be good for you.
You don't have to make yourself <u>sick</u>. You do need to make yourself a bit <u>sweaty</u> and out of
breath. If you do about <u>half an hour</u> of proper exercise <u>three times</u> a <u>week</u>, you'll be doing fine.

If you're <u>out of shape</u>, do a <u>little bit</u> of exercise <u>each day</u>. <u>Gradually increase</u> the
amount you do — don't get off the sofa and try to run 10 miles on the first day.

Find something you <u>really like doing</u>, otherwise you'll always find an excuse for not getting
around to it. If you don't want to do <u>team sport</u> or you're scared of making a <u>twit</u> of yourself
at the <u>gym</u>, try something a bit different like <u>yoga</u>, <u>dancing</u> or just going for <u>bike rides</u>.

> Get plenty of '<u>accidental exercise</u>' too —
> 1)   <u>Walk</u> instead of getting the bus.
> 2)   Don't use <u>lifts</u> (unless you're visiting Canary Wharf).
> 3)   <u>Throw away</u> the remote control!

> Keep it safe — do <u>warm up</u> and <u>stretching</u>
> exercises first, and cool-down stretches
> afterwards. Otherwise, you'll strain something.
> Don't push yourself <u>too far</u> the first time, either.

FACT: Exercise Makes You *Happy*

Yes it's true — exercise makes you feel <u>really great</u>, especially if you've been a bit down.
It <u>wakes you up</u>, takes your <u>mind</u> off other stuff and makes you feel <u>good about yourself</u>.

You'll <u>feel fab</u> — exercise makes your brain let off chemicals called
<u>endorphins</u>, and they make you feel <u>happy</u> and relaxed. Sport and
exercise definitely relieve <u>stress</u> and brush off <u>depression</u>.

It helps you <u>look good</u> — your muscles will start to get
<u>firmer</u> and <u>trimmer</u>, and it'll help you stand up <u>straighter</u> —
which makes you <u>less likely</u> to get <u>back pains</u>.

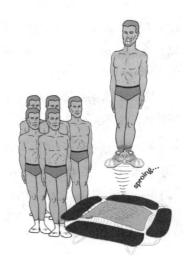

sproing...

And there's another big bonus — exercising helps you <u>burn
more energy</u>, so you can get away with <u>eating more</u> —
or actually <u>lose weight</u> if you don't change how much you eat.

If it <u>seems</u> knackering at first, <u>keep at it</u> — you'll suddenly find
you have <u>more energy</u> than ever before. It even gets to be a
lot less of a pain and (gasp!) <u>fun</u>, as your fitness improves.

Exercise Helps You *Sleep* — *which is* *Great*

Sleep isn't just something you do because there's nothing good on telly — your body <u>needs</u> to go to sleep
every <u>twenty-four hours</u> or so, otherwise it'll be <u>worn out</u>. Having plenty of <u>sleep</u> puts you in better shape to
<u>fight off diseases</u> (and pass Exams) and means you're <u>less likely</u> to get <u>stressed</u> or depressed.

Athlete's foot — just over twelve inches...

If you already do <u>three</u> lots of <u>sweat-inducing exercise</u> a week, I probably don't need to tell you any
of this. Read the page again and write down <u>three plus points</u> to exercising.

Cancer and Meningitis

Alright, here are two things to watch out for. <u>Meningitis</u> is deadly serious and comes on quickly. <u>Cancer</u> lies in wait and gets you later, but you stand a better chance if it's spotted and treated early.

Meningitis Starts like Flu — but it Can Kill You

Meningitis affects your <u>brain</u> and <u>spinal cord</u> — which means it's very dangerous.
Look out for these things:

You've got a really <u>bad headache</u>.

You've got a <u>stiff neck</u>.

You've got a <u>high temperature and fever</u>.

You're <u>vomiting</u>.

You <u>can't stand bright lights</u> (or even the TV).

You have a <u>rash</u> (which <u>doesn't go away</u> when you <u>press it</u> with a <u>glass</u>).

Meningitis can be spread by coughing/sneezing/snogging. If it's going around, there's <u>no sure way</u> to <u>avoid it</u>.

If you've got more than three of these symptoms, call the doctor or go to hospital <u>straight away</u>. Remember, it can <u>kill you</u>, so <u>don't hang about</u>.

Glandular Fever Knocks You Out for Weeks

Glandular fever <u>isn't</u> really <u>serious</u> — it just makes you knackered for about a month.
You get it from coughing/sneezing/snogging — it used to be called the 'kissing disease'.
If you've got a <u>sore throat</u>, <u>swollen glands</u> and <u>flu</u> symptoms — go to the doctor. If you've got the <u>meningitis</u> symptoms, don't brush it off as "just glandular fever" — <u>get to the doctor quick</u>.

Watch out for Cancer — It Might Kill You Later

Get into the habit of checking your <u>breasts</u> or <u>testicles</u> for <u>lumps</u> — anything new or painful.

If a <u>mole</u> on your skin <u>changes shape</u>, gets a lot <u>bigger</u> or <u>starts</u> <u>itching</u> or <u>bleeding</u>, let a doctor have a look at it — it could be serious.

Skin Cancer is a Long Term Risk of Sunbathing

Everyone knows about <u>sunburn</u> and <u>peeling skin</u> — it's no fun at all.
Even worse than sunburn, the sun can damage your skin cells and
eventually cause nasty <u>tumours</u> (cancer) on your skin.

Sunbathing also <u>ages your skin</u> and gives you loads of <u>leathery wrinkles</u>. Lovely.

This is <u>easy</u> to deal with — don't lie around in the sun for
hours on end in the nearly-nude. Try <u>not to sunbathe</u> at all
around <u>lunchtime</u> because that's when you get <u>most burnt</u>.

If you're <u>white</u>, use a <u>strong</u> sun lotion, like SPF 15, and if you're <u>ginger-haired</u> and <u>freckly</u>, stick with an SPF 20 sun lotion and cover up with a T-shirt and a hat. If you have a <u>darker</u> skin you should put a <u>low</u> protection sun cream on.

Don't let the sun go down on me...

Diseases like meningitis and cancer may be <u>rare</u>, but they're <u>deadly serious</u>. Scribble a quick list of the <u>symptoms</u> of meningitis — it'll be worth your while <u>learning</u> them too. Remember, it's a <u>killer</u>.

Dealing With Doctors

Most doctors are friendly, helpful and generally ace. Unfortunately, some doctors can be awkward. This page tells you what help you can expect from your doctor, and what to do if you're not happy.

It's Your Doctor's Job to Help You

Your doctor will help you decide what's best for you.

Don't be afraid to ask your doctor questions about what's up with you.

Your doctor should explain exactly what your treatment is going to involve. If you don't understand what they're on about, ask them to explain it again more clearly. It's part of their job — so they shouldn't mind doing it.

It's not worth going to the doctor with ordinary colds or sore throats. They go away by themselves. Also, there's no quick cure for the common cold — don't demand antibiotics, they'll be useless.

The Doctor Won't Tell Your Parents Everything

Your GP will only talk to your parents about you if you're under 16 and he or she thinks you don't understand whatever it is that he or she wants to explain to you.

If you're still worried, you've got a couple of choices:

1) If it's a sexually transmitted infection, you can go to a GUM (genito-urinary medicine) clinic. They'll definitely keep everything to themselves.

2) If you want contraception advice, or you think you might be pregnant, you can go to a family planning clinic.

You Can Find Out Medical Information from Helplines

The NHS Direct helpline is staffed by nurses. When you call them, they ask for basic information on what's wrong with you. They'll tell you whether to get something from the chemist, see your GP, call your GP out to your house or go straight to hospital — based on how serious your problem is.

There's also an NHS Direct Website (www.nhsdirect.nhs.uk) with tons of information about health.

Your local chemist can give excellent advice on minor illnesses. Ask at the pharmacy counter.

There are helplines and websites for all sorts of diseases and medical conditions. Remember, looking stuff up on the internet is helpful, but there'll be times when you need to see an actual doctor.

You Can Change Your Doctor if You Want To

Most people never need to change their doctor. You might decide to change if you really don't agree on what treatment you need, or if you want a doctor of your sex or the opposite sex, or if you don't get on with your doctor.

If your doctor shares a practice with other doctors, you could ask to see one of them instead, or ask friends what the other doctors in your area are like.

If you decide you definitely want to change your doctor, phone another surgery in your area and ask if you can join. You don't have to explain why to your old doctor or the new one.

Put your favourite doctor joke here...

It's really important to get good medical advice. There's no need to be scared of doctors — it's their job to help you out. And don't forget the other places you can get medical advice from too.

A Bit About First Aid

Alright, so it's not <u>every day</u> that one of your mates <u>falls off a cliff</u>, or <u>chokes</u> half to death on a chip. But if they did, and there was nothing you could do to help them, it'd be pretty <u>awful</u>.

If Something goes Wrong Get Help Right Away

GET HELP Dial 999... ...or <u>scream</u> or <u>shout</u> — whatever it takes. If there are two of you, one should stay with the person in trouble.

FIND OUT WHAT'S WRONG <u>Speak</u> to the person who's in trouble, or if they're <u>unconscious</u> try and work out what happened.

DON'T MAKE THINGS WORSE If you're <u>sure</u> you <u>know how to help</u> then do. But don't steam in and make the person worse, or hurt yourself. **NEVER** move someone with head or spine injuries.

Basic First Aid Really Does Save Lives

1) Someone who's <u>unconscious</u> may need their heart and lungs kick-started. The point of this is to keep them alive until the ambulance gets there, not to make them suddenly come back to life.

Mouth-to-mouth

1) *Check mouth for obstructions.*
2) *Tilt head back, open mouth, and pinch nose shut.*
3) *Breathe in, press your mouth onto theirs, slowly breathe out into their mouth.*
4) *Watch to see their chest rise.*

5) *Lift your mouth off theirs and let their chest drop. Repeat.*

Chest compressions

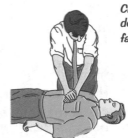

Clasp your hands and push down on their chest, a bit faster than once a second.

Do 15 chest pushes, then two mouth-to-mouth breaths. Repeat.

Check for signs of circulation.

2) Moving somebody with an <u>injured back</u> or <u>spine</u> could paralyse them.

3) If someone's <u>choking</u>, slap them hard on the back a few times. If that doesn't work, stand behind them, clasp your hands over their belly and pull up under the ribs. Get them to <u>cough</u> at the same time.

4) <u>Losing a lot of blood</u> is dangerous. You have to stop the blood pouring out — even if you have to use your best new shirt to do it. Press quite hard on the wound, and <u>keep pressing</u>.

5) Somebody having an <u>asthma attack</u> needs their inhaler fast. People who're allergic to stuff like peanuts carry a syringe to get them over their <u>allergic reaction</u>. Get the <u>inhaler</u> or <u>syringe</u> and <u>get help</u>.

6) Someone who's had an <u>electric shock</u> could give you one — don't touch them directly. Turn off the mains if you can. Use something that <u>doesn't conduct electricity</u> to get them <u>away</u> from the <u>electricity</u>.

The Best Thing is to Go on a First Aid Course

You <u>can't</u> really learn first aid from a book. The best thing you can do is go on a <u>first aid course</u> — then you can <u>help</u> when something goes wrong.

Look up the local <u>St. John Ambulance</u>, or see if you can get your <u>school</u> to organise something.

First Aid saves lives — LEARN how to do it...

I can't stress this enough — GO AND GET PROPER FIRST AID TRAINING. If you're <u>ever</u> in a situation where you could <u>save someone's life</u> instead of <u>watching them die</u>, it'll be worth it.

Eating

You can't make hard 'n' fast <u>rules</u> about how much to eat. It <u>varies</u> from person to person.

Eat When You're Hungry

There's a <u>revolutionary idea</u> if ever I heard one. Your <u>body</u> is generally <u>pretty good</u> at working out when it needs food.

Now, there are really <u>three parts</u> to this:

1) <u>Eat</u> when you're <u>hungry</u>, <u>not</u> when you're <u>bored</u> or <u>depressed</u>.

2) When you're hungry, <u>eat something</u>. Don't hold off until <u>later</u>. There's <u>nothing superheroic</u> about being able to last without food.

3) Eat <u>slowly</u>, and <u>stop</u> when you're <u>full</u> — eating at <u>breakneck speed</u> makes it harder to tell when you're full. Give your body time to work it out.

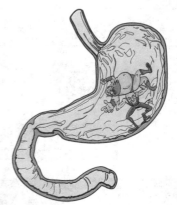

Eat Meals — and Snacks

<u>Teenagers</u> need a lot <u>more energy</u> than adults, so you'll need to eat <u>more</u> than your mum and dad.

You'll need to get some <u>decent meals</u> inside you. <u>Stodge</u> like bread, pasta, potatoes, rice, porridge and cereal keeps you going for longest.

You might need to have some <u>snacks</u> as well. Eating between meals is OK. Mind you, if you lived on <u>nothing</u> but <u>sweet</u> or <u>greasy</u> snack food like <u>chocolate</u> or crisps, you wouldn't get everything your body needed.

Here's something to make you think — if you want to pass your Exams, get some <u>food</u> inside you. Your <u>brain needs energy</u> to work properly. <u>Skipping breakfast</u> makes you <u>thick</u> — it's official.

Not Every Single Meal Needs to be Perfect

Not every meal needs to be <u>perfectly balanced</u>, so <u>don't stress</u> about it. Actually, there <u>isn't</u> one perfect meal that everyone should eat to be healthy.

It doesn't matter if you don't have <u>exactly</u> the same amount to eat every day. Just make sure it <u>balances out</u> over <u>several days</u>.

Can we swap now?

There are a lot of <u>myths</u> and <u>scare stories</u> about what foods are healthy and what foods aren't. Don't read too much into them. One thing's certain — obsessing over food is <u>definitely</u> unhealthy.

Food is food — it's not <u>capable</u> of being <u>good</u> or <u>evil</u>. After all — apples don't go around wearing little <u>halos</u> and singing hymns. Cakes don't have little <u>devil's horns</u> and pitchforks.

Healthy eating — no need to make a meal of it ...

The most <u>important</u> thing here is also the simplest — <u>eat</u> when you're <u>hungry</u>. Don't worry about every little thing you put into your mouth, either — and definitely <u>don't believe</u> the scare stories.

Thin, Fat and Diets

If you're worried about your weight, there's some good news here.

Attractiveness is Not about Size

Attractiveness is about an awful lot more than what side of the thin/fat line you're on.

In the real world, personality, self-confidence, and things like clean clothes are far more important then your exact waist measurement in inches and centimetres.

Extra inches or kilos doesn't automatically mean fat. Some people are meant to be short and wide, some are meant to be skinny and some are built like brick outhouses.

You can't change your natural body shape any more than you can change your height. You can lose extra fat if you need to.

No matter what your body shape, someone will find you attractive.

Crash Diets are Pointless and Dangerous

1) Cutting out any sort of food (eg carbohydrate or protein), or dramatically cutting down how much you eat is dangerous. Anyway, if you lose weight quickly you put it back on quickly — with interest, GUARANTEED.

2) Smoking doesn't help you lose weight, and it's worse for you than being overweight.

3) Taking 'diet pills' or laxatives to lose weight is downright reckless. People have died of it.

4) Yo-yo dieting — dieting, gaining weight, then dieting again — will end up making you look saggy and ill.

If You Want to Diet — Be Sensible

Always remember that teenagers need more energy than adults.
If you follow a weight loss diet designed for adults, you'll be overdoing it.

Find out if you really are overweight before you start dieting.
Most teenagers aren't unhealthily fat or unhealthily thin.

Too fat can be very unhealthy. Too thin can be unhealthy, too.
When you're too thin you've got no energy, you can't concentrate, and you can't fight illness. Sex hormone levels drop for boys and girls.

Cut down a little on the amount you eat at each meal.
Eat less fat. Do more exercise every day.

The fresh air diet — it'll suck the life out of you...

There are more important things than weight to worry about, but sometimes it's hard to see that. Scribble a list of reasons why dieting can be dangerous — and why being thin isn't always healthy.

Eating Healthy Stuff

If you eat a load of <u>rubbish</u> you'll <u>feel ropy</u>, and probably <u>look ropy</u> too. There's no <u>big mystery</u> to healthy eating. You just need to know the <u>facts</u> about what different foods do to your body.

Variety — That's what You Need

There's an old saying that goes "A <u>little bit</u> of what you <u>fancy</u> does you <u>good</u>." There's another one that goes "Everything in moderation." There's a lot of good sense in both of them.

If you <u>fancy</u> a bit of <u>chocolate</u>, have a little chocolate. Feeling <u>guilty</u> about eating the chocolate is actually <u>worse</u> for your health than eating just a little bit of fat and sugar. You shouldn't go overboard either — eating bar after bar after bar of chocolate <u>isn't sensible</u>.

Try not to <u>pig out</u> on <u>one</u> type of food — and if you do, don't make a <u>habit</u> of it.

This is the Fabled 'Balanced' Diet

1) OK — you need to eat some kind of <u>starchy food</u>, like rice, bread, potatoes or cereal. It's pretty darn hard to have an <u>actual meal</u> without including that kind of food.

2) You also need some kind of <u>protein</u>. <u>Meat</u> and <u>fish</u> give you protein. So does <u>dairy</u> food — milk, yoghurt and cheese. <u>Beans</u>, <u>lentils</u> and <u>nuts</u> have protein, too, and there's some protein in fruit and vegetables — good news for the <u>vegetarians</u> out there.

3) <u>Fruit</u> and <u>veg</u> have loads of <u>vitamins</u> and other <u>exciting chemicals</u> that keep your body ticking over. They're also full of <u>water</u>, which you need. Lastly, fruit and veg have plenty of <u>fibre</u>, which saves you from the <u>torture</u> of <u>constipation</u>.

4) Every single bit of your body needs <u>water</u>. It doesn't have to come from a designer bottle — <u>tap water</u> or squash will do fine. When you're drinking <u>enough</u> your pee's the colour of <u>champagne</u>.

5) You need <u>some fat</u> for insulation, but not much. There's fat in <u>meat</u>, <u>cheese</u>, <u>cakes</u> and biscuits as well as in <u>butter</u>, marge and cooking oil. <u>Sugar</u> and <u>starch</u> get stored as fat if your body doesn't use them up.

These are the Proportions — They Don't Have to be Exact

Actually, a <u>home-made burger</u> in a <u>bun</u> with <u>salad</u> will give you the <u>right mix</u> of foods. (Burgers from a <u>fast food place</u> tend to be <u>heavy</u> on <u>fat</u> and <u>light</u> on <u>vegetables</u>.)

Make about a third of what you eat the <u>starchy</u> stodgy stuff.

Another third or so should be <u>fruit and vegetables</u>. Try to eat <u>5 portions</u> of fruit and veg a day (a big spoonful counts as a portion).

<u>Dairy foods</u> should be roughly one sixth of what you eat.

Eat the same amount of meat, fish or other <u>protein</u>-packed food as dairy food.

You'll hear loads of figures for how much <u>water</u> to drink per day. You'll be <u>fine</u> if you drink a <u>glass of water</u>, squash or juice with <u>meals</u> and <u>drink</u> when you're <u>thirsty</u> — it's common sense.

You hardly <u>need</u> any sweet <u>sugary foods</u> — only about half the amount of dairy foods and meat.

Here's some food for thought...

It's not worth worrying yourself <u>sick</u> about what you eat — just use some <u>common sense</u>. Think about <u>your own diet</u> — make sure it's <u>balanced</u> and that you get plenty of <u>variety</u>.

Learn To Cook

Here's something to chew on — <u>knowing</u> how to <u>cook</u> is <u>better</u> than <u>not knowing</u> how to cook.

Get in the Kitchen and Rustle Up Some Grub

If you've never learnt to cook, <u>NOW IS THE TIME</u>. I don't mean <u>fancy</u> TV chef-style food, just the ordinary <u>simple stuff</u>. There are several top reasons for getting some hands-on action in the kitchen.

1) It's messy and a bit of a <u>laugh</u> — <u>even</u> when it goes wrong.

2) It's <u>dead quick</u> and <u>easy</u> to make (gasp!) <u>real food</u>.

3) Home-cooked food is <u>healthier</u> than pre-packaged food. It has more <u>vitamins</u> and <u>minerals</u> in and <u>less artificial gunk</u>, <u>less fat</u> and <u>less sugar</u>.

4) It's way, way <u>cheaper</u> to make almost anything you can think of from scratch.

5) Some of the most unlikely people turn out to be <u>brilliant</u> cooks — it could be your <u>hidden talent</u>.

6) <u>Last</u> but not at all least — talented chef-ing <u>impresses</u> the fellas/ladies (delete as applicable).

Get a <u>book</u> and <u>have a go</u>.

Check through the recipe <u>before</u> you start — you don't want to find out that you haven't got a <u>really important</u> ingredient when you're already <u>halfway</u> through.

Dirty Kitchens Give You the Squits — Raw Meat is Worst

There are some fairly basic <u>DOs</u> and <u>DON'Ts</u> for kitchen hygiene. Avoid giving yourself <u>food poisoning</u> and — just as importantly — don't give it to other people.

You've GOT to...

Keep the kitchen <u>clean</u> so bacteria <u>can't breed</u> in spills and leftovers.

<u>Check the packet</u> to see whether food's meant to be in the fridge or freezer.

<u>Wash your hands</u> before you eat or cook.

But...

NEVER...
...let <u>raw meat</u> (or meaty hands, knives, chopping boards, etc.) <u>touch</u> any food that's <u>cooked</u>, or gets eaten <u>raw</u>, like salad. Bacteria from the meat will get onto the cooked stuff.

NEVER...
...eat food that's <u>gone past</u> the <u>use-by date</u> — it's there for a reason.

NEVER...
...eat food that <u>looks</u> or <u>smells</u> <u>off</u> — not that you ever would.

If you don't think this stuff matters, think about staying up all night <u>trotting to the bathroom</u>.

Cooking with an old egg — you can't beat it...

No two ways about it — cooking at home is <u>good fun</u> and you really can't go far wrong. When was the last time <u>you tried</u> cooking... if it was ages ago then it must be time to <u>give it a shot</u> again.

Respecting People

This is about how to make your life <u>easier</u>. You'd be surprised how much <u>hassle</u> can be avoided by giving people <u>respect</u>, and by making sure <u>you get it</u> in return.

Everyone Deserves Respect

1) Like d'oh — treat other people the way <u>you'd want</u> to be treated. The best way to <u>get</u> respect from folk is to <u>show them</u> some respect in the first place.

2) Treating people like <u>dirt</u> will only make them <u>dislike</u> you. It won't get you any <u>real respect</u> in the long run.

Don't Pick On Things People Can't Change

It <u>doesn't matter</u> if it's something <u>serious</u> like skin colour, sexuality or gender, or something <u>dumb</u> like a person's height or the clothes they're wearing:

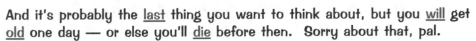

> Don't pick on other people — give them a bit of respect

Let's be clear — if you pick on people, you're gonna wind up in a heck of a lot of <u>hassle</u>: at home, at school or with the police. It's just <u>not worth it</u>.

Remember — there are probably things about <u>you</u> that other people don't like. That <u>doesn't</u> give <u>them</u> the right to give you <u>personal grief</u> about it.

Some of These Things Will Happen to You

It can seem like a bit of a laugh — taking the mick out of old people, or the disabled. But just remember, <u>you</u> might end up <u>disabled</u> one day — from a sports injury or a car crash, perhaps.

And it's probably the <u>last</u> thing you want to think about, but you <u>will</u> get <u>old</u> one day — or else you'll <u>die</u> before then. Sorry about that, pal.

Disabled people aren't stupid — and neither are old people. Maybe Grandad's a bit <u>deaf</u> and Grandma walks a bit <u>slowly</u>, but that has <u>nothing</u> to do with their <u>mental abilities</u>.

> They deserve as much respect as anyone else

Enjoy Your Own Life — Don't Worry About Other People's

<u>Picking on</u> folk or <u>hating</u> them is <u>bad</u> for you. You end up causing <u>yourself</u> a ton of <u>needless aggro</u>. Spend your time <u>enjoying your own life</u> — not giving other people hassle about theirs.

Treating people badly — it's not worth the bother...

I dunno, it's just not <u>worth</u> treating people like dirt. It's like <u>creating</u> all this <u>extra hassle</u> for yourself. D'you really want to make <u>hundreds of enemies</u> just by being a <u>nasty piece of work</u>...

Dealing with People

It's all very well talking about respect — but what does it mean in practice...
Well, it's about how you deal with people — the way you act when you're around them.

Don't Get Sucked into Deliberate Bullying

Bullying is dishing out any kind of bad treatment — hitting or pushing people, deliberately getting them in trouble, name-calling or even stealing their stuff and demanding cash.

It doesn't matter why you're doing it — it's bang out of order. If it's being done for racist or homophobic reasons, then it's even more serious.

If you or your mates get caught bullying, you could find yourself in serious grief. This is one situation where it's definitely not so hot to follow the crowd.

Peer Pressure's a Lot Like Bullying

Oh dear, it's one of those yawnsome PSHE phrases again. All peer pressure means is when you feel pressured to do stuff to be cool with your mates (your 'peers').

Most of the time it's a bit daft but fairly harmless — you feel pressured to wear the same fashions or listen to the same tunes. But you can also end up doing stuff you actually don't want to — like bullying people, getting in fights or trying drugs.

The secret is to stand up for yourself. Following the crowd like a sheep doesn't make anybody big and hard — it just shows how insecure they are. Being yourself and doing what you want will actually make your life more fun in the long run.

Don't Be a Doormat — You Deserve Some Respect

Be confident. That doesn't mean being arrogant or cocky — it means being OK with yourself. There's no point in rushing to change yourself just to suit other people.

Often, standing up for yourself and being sure of what you want (and what you don't want) can earn you a lot of respect from other people.

Remember — You Can Offend People By Accident

You're not going to get through life without offending someone somewhere. You can be the nicest person in the world and you'll still say something wrong or insulting from time to time.

The thing is, it's all about how you deal with it. Even if you genuinely thought you were right, you should still be prepared to admit you were wrong. Be ready to apologise too — it won't make you any less of a strong person. In fact, it makes you more of one.

"So you're saying that now we're teenagers we can take a fence for no obvious reason. Brilliant!"

Where do you draw the line...

None of us is perfect — we're all gonna say stupid things. But we've all got a mind of our own — next time you're teasing somebody, think how it would make you feel to be on the receiving end.

Dealing with Trouble

No matter how much you try to avoid it, there's always a <u>chance</u> you might find yourself in trouble. But if you <u>use your head</u> and a bit of <u>common sense</u>, you'll be absolutely fine.

You Can Deal with Trouble — with Common Sense

It doesn't matter if it's bullying or teasing — any kind of trouble is <u>downright nasty</u> if it happens to you. The trick is <u>not</u> to get sucked into trying to <u>fight back</u> and making things <u>worse</u>.

The best way to deal with it is <u>common sense</u>. If you can <u>avoid</u> it, try to <u>steer clear</u> of hassle. If it's something <u>more serious</u>, like racist or homophobic bullying, then you've really <u>got</u> to tell someone about it, no matter how hard that's gonna be.

D'oh!

> Try and <u>steer clear</u> of trouble — but if that doesn't work just <u>TELL SOMEONE</u>!

If it's Racist or Prejudiced then Report it Pronto

Any kind of <u>racist</u>, <u>sexist</u> or <u>homophobic</u> bullying is way out of line — whether it's making a few <u>jokes</u> or <u>attacking people</u> in the street. It needs to be stopped — which means telling someone.

Find someone you <u>trust</u> — like a teacher or whoever and just <u>explain</u> what's going on. If you're worried they won't take you seriously, have a look at some internet resources like <u>Bullying Online</u> (www.bullying.co.uk). They'll give you <u>advice</u> on what to do.

I know it's hard, but it <u>isn't</u> telling tales — no one has to take this sort of thing.

Use Your Head — Try to Avoid Any Sort of Bullying

Right, if you're being bullied, here are some things that could help.

1) Stick <u>with other people</u> whenever you feel under threat — bullies hate witnesses.

2) Vary your <u>route</u> home to <u>avoid ambushes</u>. Sit <u>near the driver</u> on a bus.

3) Try to <u>make friends</u>. Chances are <u>other people</u> are being bullied by the same person — the <u>more</u> of you there are in a group, the <u>less likely</u> you are to get bullied.

4) If you're being sent <u>threatening text messages</u> or <u>emails</u>, it's a CRIMINAL OFFENCE. Report it to the police, or tell someone in authority, like a teacher.

5) <u>Tell someone</u> what's happening. If the person you tell <u>doesn't understand</u> how you feel about the bullying, <u>don't give up</u> — keep on trying or talk to <u>someone else</u>.

Violence Isn't the Answer

It's <u>tempting</u> to try to fight back — but you could end up in serious bother. First of all, the people giving you trouble may <u>grass on you</u> for attacking them. How <u>stupid</u> would that be...

Secondly, if you and <u>your mates</u> go after them, <u>their mates</u> may come back after <u>you</u>. Before you know it, things will get <u>very ugly</u> indeed. You don't need to make <u>more enemies</u>.

One more thing — don't <u>ever</u> carry <u>weapons</u> for 'protection'. It'll just make things far worse.

You don't need to be violent to stay out of trouble...

Touch wood, you'll <u>hardly ever</u> need this stuff — but it's worth storing away <u>just in case</u> you do.

Surviving Home Life

Part of looking after yourself is how you survive <u>at home</u>. There are all sorts of <u>problems</u> that can turn up sooner or later in any family — and some of them can be a <u>nightmare</u> to deal with.

Sometimes Family Life Sucks

Mom, if you love me <u>that</u> much...
...what's with all the semolina?

The trouble with families is they can be full of people who <u>don't understand each other</u>. Let's face it — your friends are the people you <u>choose</u> to hang out with, but you're <u>stuck</u> with your family.

There's always going to be <u>some conflict</u> in families — arguments, sulking and downright frustration are <u>totally normal</u>. Almost all parents <u>really love</u> their kids — but they don't often <u>understand them</u>. And vice versa...

Communicating is Dead Important in Families

No shock, Sherlock — <u>bottling stuff</u> up makes things <u>worse</u>. But families can be tricky to talk to.

Alright... alright... I'm SORRY!

<u>Listen</u> to what other people have to say — even if you think it's wrong.
<u>Being honest</u> usually makes life easier in the end — keeping secrets can often backfire big time.
<u>Don't</u> start <u>accusing</u> or <u>insulting</u> people — it'll make things worse.
<u>Say sorry</u> if you've done something wrong or hurt someone.
<u>Be positive</u> — try to suggest a positive solution.

Breaking Big News isn't Easy

If you have <u>big news</u> to tell, like coming out or that you're pregnant, then do it <u>gently</u> — don't just blurt it out. It may help to talk over <u>how to do it</u> with someone <u>neutral</u> first.

Don't expect a parade — it could take <u>time</u> for people to accept the news. Sometimes there's <u>no right time</u> to say things, but people can be <u>more hurt</u> if they find out your secrets <u>later</u>.

Divorce Can Feel Like the End of the World

<u>Divorce</u> is horrible — and it's getting more and more common.

When your parents <u>split up</u> it can be awful. There'll probably be lots of rowing, and your parents may even try to make you take sides. <u>Don't blame yourself</u> or them — things <u>change</u> a lot and it takes time to get <u>used</u> to it and <u>get over it</u>.

There <u>isn't</u> an easy answer to make the problems go away — divorce can make you miserable with your friends, your schoolwork and everything. Try to talk to someone about <u>how you feel</u>, or phone Childline free on 0800 11 11. And keep thinking it <u>will get better</u> — it's <u>not your fault</u> and your parents do <u>still love you</u>. They're <u>still</u> your parents after all.

Families — can't live with 'em, can't live without 'em...

Families — who needs them. Surviving <u>home life</u> can be a challenge — but it's easier to live through if you can <u>talk</u> to the people around you, even about difficult stuff like <u>divorce</u>.

Keeping Safe

This page is all about common sense — how to stay out of trouble whenever you can.

There are Some Evil People Out There

Most people you meet in life will be lovely. Fantastic. Some others will really get up your nose, but you'll be able to deal with them. But it pays to remember that there are some very nasty people out there. And you can't just trust everybody you meet.

Don't hide away, but do be aware of the possible dangers — if you act pretty smart and don't take stupid chances, you'll be fine.

Just follow me my dear...

Keeping Safe's About Using Your Head

1) Walk home along lighted streets with other people whenever you can.

2) If you're alone on a dark street and someone else comes along behind you, cross to the opposite side. They should keep their distance — if they don't, call for help. (If you're a bloke walking behind a woman, she might be scared you're following her. Crossing the road puts her mind at rest.)

3) If a stranger asks you to go with them, for Pete's sake don't go — especially if it's a lift in a car.

4) Remember — if you get drunk you can find yourself doing things you wouldn't normally do. Also, watch out for people trying to spike your drinks in pubs — trying to add drugs or something.

5) Think before you leave a party or go somewhere quiet with people you've only just met.

6) If it makes you feel better, carry a personal alarm — they're darn loud and dead effective at scaring people off. If you don't have an alarm and you get attacked, shout "FIRE!", never "RAPE!" — for some weird reason people tend to ignore shouts of "Rape!", but they flock to fire.

7) Don't give personal details in internet chatrooms, especially not addresses or home phone numbers — you don't know who you're online with. That "16-year old Britney lookalike" could easily be a 48-year old perv called Brian. And don't arrange meetings without telling your parents.

Always Let Someone Know Where You Are

Yeah — it's a real chore telling people where you're going — especially if you don't really want them to know exactly what you're up to.

> Excuse me sir, your mother thought you might be feeling the cold.

It's dead important though — and it doesn't matter who you tell as long as they're responsible, like a brother or sister, or a willing older mate.

All you have to do is say where you'll be, and when you'll be back. If you'll be late then give them a ring. You know you're safe at your mate's house, but if you're not home when you said, your mum'll think you're dead in a ditch.

Maybe it sounds pretty embarrassing, phoning in like that —but it's a lot less embarrassing than having the police turn up at your mate's party because your Mum's worried about you. You could even just text, that way your friends won't even know who you are on the phone to.

Common sense — it's blummin' obvious really...

This isn't supposed to panic you — the chances of running into big trouble really are pretty darned tootin' slim. If you use your head and think about what you do, you should stay safe.

Abuse

This is another one of those hush-hush topics that no one likes talking about.
It's horribly serious, I'm afraid, and you really do need to know about it.

Abuse is when Someone Takes Advantage

Abuse is when someone tries to take advantage of another person — either by hitting or hurting them, threatening them or doing sexual things to them against their will.

Forget what you've heard — it isn't just about dirty old men and young girls. This sort of thing can happen to anyone at any age, and it can happen at home or at school — so be careful.

Most Abusers are People the Victim Knows

Incredible, isn't it... most violent or sexual attacks are done by relatives or friends of the victim. It's one reason why they can be difficult to detect — victims are afraid of speaking out in case no one believes them, or the attacker has threatened to harm them if they tell anyone.

Any Abuse is Wrong and Needs to be Stopped

It takes real guts for someone to come forward and say what's going on.

- It's really important that any violence or dodgy sex stuff is reported — whether it happens at home or anywhere else.

- Neglecting children — not giving them food, water, shelter and clean clothes — is also a kind of abuse. Not having the best brand of trainers isn't abuse. Not having any shoes at all could be abuse.

- Look out for your friends — if they get withdrawn or tearful or start acting oddly, ask them gently what's going on. Do it carefully — they may refuse to tell you, or even get angry. Don't jump to conclusions, but if you get suspicious then tell someone you trust.

- Telling a teacher or the police isn't snitching — it could be saving someone's life. And don't let anyone fob you off — if you're sure it's true, they've got a duty to sort it out.

- There are loads of confidential organisations you can talk to if you're worried about something or someone. They'll give advice and see that the situation gets sorted.

- The NSPCC is the Society for the Prevention of Cruelty to Children — their helpline is 0808 800 5000, and their e-mail address is help@nspcc.org.uk.

- Childline was set up to help children in danger. Their free phone number is 0800 11 11.

Remember — None of It is the Victim's Fault

The effects of sex attacks or violence can stay with someone for life — it can feel like they're to blame for what happened. But it isn't their fault. Over time, with counselling they can start to deal with what was done to them.

Fortunately, most people grow up without experiencing any abuse. But that shouldn't mean you don't take it seriously.

It's not smart to accuse someone just to get back at them — it's wasting time that could be spent helping somebody who really is being abused.

Too important to ignore...

It's really important to tell someone if you're worried about yourself or another person.

Running Away

It sounds like an <u>easy</u> way out, running away — but it's a lot <u>more trouble</u> than you'd think.

People Run Away for All Sorts of Reasons

1) When they're worried about being <u>abused</u> at home or at school.
2) After a big <u>row</u> at home — for whatever reason it may be.
3) If their parents threaten to <u>throw them out</u>.
4) When they've had enough and decide they want their <u>independence</u>.
5) Because they're <u>bored</u> with their lives.
6) If they've done something wrong and want to try to <u>escape</u> from it.

Running Away's Not as Smart as It Seems

The problem with running away is it doesn't <u>solve</u> much — and causes a whole lot of <u>new grief</u>. For a start, anyone <u>under 16</u> will have the police looking for them because they're under-age.

Then there's the problem of <u>where to stay</u>. Staying with friends <u>isn't</u> gonna be permanent, and living on the street is a <u>nightmare</u>. Getting council accommodation <u>takes time</u> — and you may get referred to social services instead of getting the nice flat you want.

<u>Money</u>'s a problem too. Even if you've got savings, they won't go far. If you don't have <u>somewhere to live</u>, you won't be able to get a <u>job</u> — which is when people end up stealing or selling sex to strangers to get cash.

Living on the Street is Just Plain Daft

There's <u>nothing cool</u> about living on the street. Most homeless people <u>don't choose</u> to do it. It's <u>seriously cold</u> — especially if you're used to a warm house. In winter it can get so cold you could <u>die</u>. It'll be <u>dirty</u> and you <u>won't</u> be able to wash. You <u>can't sleep</u> in case people <u>nick</u> your stuff — and you could get <u>robbed</u> or even <u>raped</u>. You <u>can't</u> count on getting a place in an <u>emergency shelter</u> either — they fill up quickly.

When you <u>run out</u> of money, you'll find yourself <u>starving</u> to death as well. That's when people start turning to <u>booze</u> or <u>drugs</u> to feel better (except they don't really). And that's when they get <u>desperate</u>...

Do Something Positive to Sort Your Problem

If you're <u>in danger</u> at home, tell <u>someone</u> — a trusted teacher, your doctor or whoever. You're entitled to protection and somewhere safe to live.

Or you can phone <u>SHELTER</u>, the homeless charity, on <u>0808 800 4444</u>. They'll be able to tell you what your options are and give you sensible and safe advice.

If you've just <u>had enough</u> of living at home, see if there's some way of spending a <u>short</u> time away — with a friend or relative maybe. Take time to <u>think</u> if it's <u>really</u> what you want. And <u>tell people</u> where you are.

> If you realise you've made a mistake GO HOME — sorting things out is <u>better</u> than suffering on your own.

There are better options than running away...

Living at home can be a pain — but running away <u>solves nothing</u>. In fact, often it makes things <u>worse</u>.

Revision Summary

It's time to exercise all those little grey cells again. This is the bit where you can see if you've been paying attention. It's not a test — just a few questions to get you thinking about what you've read and how it affects your life...

Questions on Section Five — Health

1) Give three good reasons for getting plenty of exercise.

2) Why do you need sleep?

3) What are the symptoms of meningitis?

4) What's the worst thing that can happen if you sunbathe too much?

5) What are your options if you need to see a doctor, but don't want to see your family GP?

6) What's the best way to learn first aid?

Questions on Section Six — Food

1) When should you eat? a) When you're hungry   b) Only ever at meal times c) Watching TV.

2) Why eat breakfast?

3) Name two things apart from weight which affect how attractive a person is?

4) Who needs more energy, teens or adults?

5) If you do need to lose weight, what's the best way to do it?

6) Give two good reasons why it's great to be able to cook.

7) Why is it important to keep food in the right place (fridge, freezer, cupboard etc.)?

Questions on Section Seven — Looking After Yourself

1) Name three things people can do to show that they respect you.

2) Give three examples of disrespectful behaviour.

3) What is bullying? Give three examples.

4) What's peer pressure?

5) What's the name of the internet resource to help people who are being bullied? What's their web address?

6) Name three practical things you could do if you were being bullied.

7) Give four things you can do to help make your home life more harmonious.

8) What's the phone number for Childline?

9) People sometimes ignore shouts of "Help!", or "Rape!". What could you shout to get more attention if you're attacked by somebody?

10) Why shouldn't you give out personal information on the internet?

Coping with Change

Some big things happen in life that you just <u>can't</u> do anything about — relationships break up, parents get divorced and people suddenly die. And something like that can really <u>screw you up</u>.

Dealing with *Divorce* and *Separation* Takes *Time*

If your parents are separating, it could affect where you live, where you go to school — any number of pretty <u>fundamental</u> things in your life. Then there's the fact that suddenly one of your parents <u>isn't there</u> all the time. It can <u>almost</u> feel like they've died.

You might be <u>surprised</u> by some of the things you feel, but <u>don't panic</u>:

> 1) You may feel angry, confused and sad all at different times — you aren't going crazy, it's a normal part of dealing with what's happened.
>
> 2) Don't blame yourself — it isn't your fault, and you don't have to try to fix it.
>
> 3) Don't worry if you don't really feel anything at all — cutting yourself off is sometimes the easiest way to cope.

Even if you're <u>lucky</u> enough to have parents who are still happily together, you'll <u>probably</u> have a friend who has to deal with <u>their</u> parents divorcing. Try and be as <u>supportive</u> as you can — but <u>don't expect</u> to be able to <u>understand</u> what they're going through.

When *Someone Dies* it's Hard to Know What to *Feel*

When someone close to you <u>dies</u> it can be awful. There's <u>no easy way</u> to cope — that person has gone from your life. At first you may not know what to feel — you may not <u>feel anything</u> at all. Later you may get <u>angry</u> with the person for dying — and feel guilty afterwards. It's <u>alright</u> to feel that.

Sometimes, when you start to <u>feel better</u> about things it <u>almost seems wrong</u>. But you <u>don't</u> have to keep feeling upset forever — <u>life goes on</u>. You <u>won't</u> <u>forget</u> the person, but you <u>will</u> be able to <u>survive</u> without them.

Don't Expect *Things to Get Better* Overnight

It <u>will get better</u> — it may not seem like it at first but it <u>will</u>.

1) Lean on each other — if your family is going through a tough time, <u>be supportive</u> and let <u>yourself</u> be supported, too. <u>Don't</u> think you have to do this <u>on your own</u>.

2) Don't brood — sitting <u>worrying</u> about things just keeps the <u>wounds open</u>. Try to keep busy and think about <u>other things</u> to give yourself time to get over it — and <u>don't</u> feel guilty about it.

Some things take time to get better...

It's weird how <u>big changes</u> in your life make you feel. They catch you <u>unawares</u>, and you find yourself confused, angry and sad all at once. Just remember it's <u>normal</u> — and it will get <u>better</u>.

Feeling Down

We all feel down sometimes, but learning to deal with it is important. Far better to write pages and pages of bad poetry than sit and stew in a miserable haze. You can help yourself feel better...

Feeling Down Sometimes is Normal

Get this clear straight away — feeling down or unhappy every now and then is totally normal. We all have times when we feel miserable, but it usually goes away again.

Depression is Much Worse

Depression is not just feeling down — it's feeling bad about yourself and your life most of the time. It's a mental illness that affects lots of people, but it's a bit tricky to describe — no one really knows what it's like unless they've had it.

Some common symptoms are:

100 thousand million tonnes

- Tired all the time
- No energy
- Panic attacks
- Less concentration
- Crying at everything
- Serious mood swings
- Always forgetting stuff
- No sleep/no decent sleep

You don't need to have the lot to be depressed — but if you have several for more than a couple of weeks then chances are you're depressed. That's when you need to get help — go to your GP.

You Can't Just Pull Yourself Together

It's not as easy as some people think — you can't just "pull yourself together". But, if you find yourself getting bogged down in life and depressed, these tips could help.

1) *Talk about your feelings* with family or friends. If you get into the *habit* of talking about what's annoying or upsetting you, then it won't eat away at you.

2) *Stay healthy* — try to *exercise* and *relax*. Some people find stuff like yoga or aromatherapy helps them, but more everyday stuff like football and tennis is fine. Don't let your depression affect your eating habits too much.

3) If you start to feel a bit *down*, try and focus on *positive things*. Thinking positive *does help*.

4) Make sure you've got something to *look forward to*. And by that I *don't* mean bingeing, whether it's on drink or drugs or spending or eating. Just do something you *really like doing*.

5) Hang around with *your friends*. Don't sit in *on your own* all the time, even if you want to.

Don't give up — even if none of these things seem to work. Keep looking for something that will.

There's actually some truth in "Look on the Bright Side"...

Thinking positive won't stop you from ever feeling down — but it will help you get through it. Just remember — if you feel really down or depressed go to a doctor. Don't suffer in silence.

Feeling Stressed

No one needs it but, yep, everyone gets stressed sometimes. It's one of those things you've just got to learn to deal with, otherwise it can do you a lot of harm.

Stress is Caused by Too Much Pressure

Stress affects all of us — it's caused by too much pressure making you feel terrible. It isn't really an illness, but it can end up making you ill.

> Stress raises your blood pressure which increases the risk of heart attacks and strokes. It also causes headaches, difficulty sleeping, or digestive problems like constipation and indigestion. It can make you angry or depressed, and it may affect how you treat people.

If You Can't Cope — Stop Pushing Yourself

Everything can be blown out of proportion when you're stressed. It's really important to take a step back from things to get some perspective. Make the effort to do something different to relax — you'll feel better for it, and it'll help you keep a balanced view of all your problems.

Think about the things that are really bothering you and then work out what the worst possible consequence could be. Chances are it wouldn't be the end of the world. Try and remember that.

Panic Attacks are Sudden Feelings of Fear

Panic attacks are like a sudden burst of intense fear. They can affect you even if you've never had one before. They'll make you dizzy, breathless, shaky and your heartbeat may become irregular.

They can be caused by stressful situations.

1)   If you're worried about having a panic attack, keep a paper bag handy.
2)   Breathe into the bag slowly and re-breathe the air. Do this at least 10 times.
3)   Remove the bag and breathe normally for a few minutes.
4)   Repeat breathing in and out of the paper bag if you need it.

Learn this and you'll know what to do if someone else has a panic attack.

Anxiety is Feeling Uneasy and Worried All the Time

Everyone feels really uneasy sometimes — but for some people it can be a constant problem. They feel restless or on edge all the time; they get tired easily; they can't concentrate or their mind goes completely blank; they're irritable and their muscles are always tensed; and they can't sleep.

Anxiety is actually really common. It can be very scary, what with dizziness, inexplicable pains and heart pounding. It's sortable, so if you have symptoms for a few weeks, go see your GP pronto. They'll be able to give you some medication which can really help — it's the same if you're having panic attacks too.

Don't let stress spoil your life — you're allowed to relax...

Stress is a pain in the bum, no mistake. It's a warning sign that you're under too much pressure — you can deal with this by taking a break. Anxiety is harder to beat by yourself — your GP can help.

Suicide & Self Harm

Many people feel <u>suicidal</u> at some time — like everything's just got too much, and no one cares if they were to die right now. But usually people get over it — when they don't, they <u>need help fast</u>.

Suicidal *Feelings* Aren't *That* Rare

There's a world of difference between <u>feeling</u> like you want to kill yourself and <u>making definite plans</u>. <u>Feeling</u> suicidal is usually a <u>temporary</u> thing.

Making <u>plans</u> to do it is a whole different kettle of fish — that's when you've <u>gotta</u> get help.

If You Feel Suicidal *Stop* and *Talk* First

It's easy to act on impulse — but it's really important to <u>stop and think</u>. You need to <u>talk to someone</u> about how you feel. It <u>doesn't</u> have to be anyone you <u>know</u>, either.

> *Ring the Samaritans — it's <u>only a local call charge</u> and <u>confidential</u>, and it <u>won't</u> <u>show up on your phone bill</u>. They'll <u>listen</u> to whatever you have to say, and they're <u>okay</u> if you <u>don't want to talk</u>. You can get them to <u>phone you back</u> if you want.*
>
> ### 08457 90 90 90 or email jo@samaritans.org
>
> *You're <u>not alone</u> — every year 50,000 teenagers speak to the Samaritans.*

You could also go and <u>see your GP</u> — though that sometimes feels harder cos you know them.

Suicide *Doesn't* Do *Anyone* Any *Favours*

Many people who try suicide are convinced they're doing their friends and family a <u>favour</u> — but they <u>aren't</u>. It's <u>absolutely devastating</u> for the people left behind — parents, family or mates.

Some suicide attempts are a cry for help — the person's so <u>desperate</u> they'll try anything. They <u>don't really</u> want to die, but they want someone to take their pain seriously.

Some people <u>want to be found</u> before they die, but often they <u>aren't</u>. It's not worth taking the risk.

You *Don't* Have to *Inflict* Your Pain on *Yourself*

Some people find a different kind of outlet for their <u>pain</u> — <u>self-harm</u>. Self-harm's when people <u>hurt themselves deliberately</u>, by <u>cutting</u> or <u>burning</u> themselves, say. It's a totally <u>different</u> thing from a <u>suicide attempt</u>.

Like all mental illnesses, the reasons for self-harm vary from person to person. But once someone starts, it's very difficult for them to stop — it's <u>addictive</u>.

People who do it <u>shouldn't</u> feel ashamed and guilty — but they should <u>talk to someone</u> who can help. <u>Counsellors</u> and <u>the Samaritans</u> are really good at dealing with this sort of thing.

If you think someone you know may be self-harming, <u>don't</u> try to <u>take control</u>. It's <u>not</u> up to you to fix it. Just keep trying to point them in the direction of <u>expert help</u> — and stay <u>supportive</u>.

The <u>wounds</u> caused by self harm can be <u>nasty</u>, so they'll definitely <u>need treating</u>, whether or not the self-harming <u>itself</u> gets treated.

Don't be afraid to talk to someone...

It's one thing to feel suicidal, and another thing to kill yourself. If you find yourself feeling suicidal for Pete's sake <u>TALK TO SOMEONE</u>. The <u>Samaritans</u> are there 24 hours: 08457 90 90 90.

Eating Disorders

Eating disorders might not seem like <u>mental health problems</u> — but <u>they are</u>, and serious ones too.

Eating Disorders Aren't Really About Food

Eating disorders generally involve people becoming <u>obsessed</u> about <u>how much</u> they are eating (and what it will do to their <u>figure</u>). These problems can start when people are <u>depressed</u> or <u>worried</u> about other things.

The problem is actually in the person's <u>head</u> — not in their stomach. It's all to do with how they <u>see themselves</u> and how they <u>think other people</u> see them. Even if they're thin they <u>think</u> they're fat — it's completely illogical.

Anorexia is When Losing Weight Gets Dangerous

Anorexia usually starts when people are <u>depressed</u> about something else. They think they're fat so they start <u>dieting</u>. Soon they <u>can't stop</u>, convinced <u>they're fat</u> even when they're painfully <u>thin</u>.

Soon you <u>can't concentrate</u> or sleep. If you're a girl you can <u>stop</u> getting periods, and if you're a bloke your sex hormone levels start to <u>drop</u>. You feel <u>cold</u> all the time, you get thinner, your hands and feet go blue, your skin gets dry and hairy on your neck, arms and legs — in fact your body starts to <u>die</u> from <u>starvation</u>.

And if it isn't treated, anorexia can <u>kill</u> — 20% of untreated cases end in <u>death</u>...

Bulimia is Binge-Eating and Making Yourself Sick

1) Bulimics obsess about their weight. They tend to see food as 'bad' and so <u>diet hard</u>.

2) Their body gets <u>desperate</u> for food until they can't stand it and <u>binge eat</u>. Then they make themselves <u>throw up</u>, or take <u>laxatives</u> to dump it out.

3) When they <u>aren't bingeing</u>, they're <u>dieting</u> — until they get hungry and <u>binge again</u>. It's a vicious circle — they end up feeling <u>guilty</u> about it but <u>can't stop</u> doing it.

All that puking <u>burns</u> throats, <u>damages</u> vocal chords and <u>rots</u> teeth — yeuch! Taking lots of <u>laxatives</u> can make you very ill. And, yep, bulimia can <u>kill</u> too.

You Can't Fix Eating Disorders On Your Own

Loads of people <u>think</u> if someone's got an eating disorder, just force them to eat. Unfortunately, it <u>isn't</u> that easy. If you really want to <u>help</u> someone with an eating problem, then:

1) Don't make food an issue — they'll feel more comfortable with you if it isn't.

2) Don't force them to talk — listen if they want to talk, but don't push them.

3) Don't change your eating habits — don't avoid eating in front of them. They need to see food is a normal part of life. But don't go out of your way to eat every time you see them either.

4) Encourage them to go to a doctor or speak to a helpline. They'll need expert help to sort this out.

It really is OK to ask for help...

Eating disorders are <u>unpleasant</u>. They're <u>not</u> about looking good or feeling sexy — they're about big <u>mental problems</u>. Anybody suffering from one needs <u>help</u> and understanding, <u>not</u> bullying.

Dealing With Mental Health

<u>Loads</u> of people get <u>mentally ill</u>, just like <u>loads</u> of people get 'normally' ill.
To be honest, it's best to think of them in the <u>same way</u> — much easier too.

If Things get Bad — See a Doctor

Most mental health problems are a bit <u>too tricky</u> for you to deal with on your own. Same way as
I wouldn't want to have to deal with someone's broken leg, or ear infection, or cancer or the like.
So the <u>best thing</u> is to find someone who <u>knows what they're doing</u> — let them sort it out.

Obviously don't go to the doctor's
cos you've had a <u>bad day</u> — it
could just be a <u>one-off</u> thing.

But if you still feel <u>constantly</u> down
after a <u>couple of weeks</u>, then <u>do go
to the doctor</u> — you need to get
better, and he or she can <u>help</u>.

Helpful People

<u>Mind</u> (mental health charity)
www.mind.org.uk

<u>Sane</u> (mental health charity)
Saneline 0845 767 8000
www.sane.org.uk

<u>Eating disorders</u>
www.anred.com

Your GP might give you <u>medication</u> to help you, or refer you to an <u>expert</u> to get things sorted.

Be There For Your Mates — Don't Try to Cure Them

If your mate has a mental problem or you're worried they might have, it <u>isn't</u> your job
to cure them — but it'll help them massively to know you're there to <u>support</u> them.

1) *Be there if they need to talk — and be ready to listen.*

2) *Don't push them — let them know you're around <u>if</u> they want to talk.*

3) *Maybe give them numbers of people to talk to, like the Samaritans.*

4) *Suggest they talk to a GP — but be prepared for them to refuse.*

5) *Don't give up on them — even if they're rude or nasty to you.*

It's something they
can't help — don't
forget, it's an <u>illness</u>.

<u>Don't blame</u> your friend for the way they're acting — especially if they're <u>extra touchy</u> with you.
If you're <u>really worried</u> talk to an <u>adult</u> you trust about what's going on — and ask for <u>advice</u>.

Things take <u>time</u> to <u>get worse</u> and <u>time</u> to <u>get better</u>. Don't expect it to get better overnight.
If things have <u>already</u> been bad for a while, your friend will need some kind of <u>help</u>.

You can't be the cure, so don't try to be...

<u>Don't</u> invent a mental health problem when nothing's wrong, but don't be <u>ashamed</u> of asking
for help if you really need it. <u>Admitting</u> you have a problem is the first step to <u>recovery</u>.

Revision Summary

Oh boy, what a section... There's a lot to take in — but it's all stuff that could come in very handy some day. I think the main thing to realise is how common some of these things are, and how important it is to get expert help. Nobody has to suffer mental health problems on their own. That's just as true if you've got problems or you have a friend who has — there is a way to make things better. Have a look at these questions now, just to get things straight in your head. Like I said before, you never know when it'll come in handy.

1) Give three examples of emotions people sometimes feel when there's been a big change in their life.
2) Give two things you could do when you're trying to cope with major change.
3) What are two differences between just feeling down and being depressed? List six common symptoms of depression.
4) What could you do to try and help yourself if you were depressed?
5) Is it normal to feel down?
6) What causes stress?
7) Give an example of one thing you can do to help you with stress, and explain how it can help.
8) How would you feel if you were having a panic attack? Name three common symptoms.
9) Why is a paper bag useful if somebody is having a panic attack?
10) What is anxiety? List at least three of its common symptoms.
11) Is it rare to have suicidal feelings?
12) Give three useful things to know about the Samaritans.
13) What's the Samaritans' phone number?
14) Give two examples of self-harming.
15) What should you do if you think someone you know is self-harming?
16) What is anorexia?
17) Name three physical symptoms of extreme anorexia.
18) What is bulimia?
19) What are the web addresses of three organisations that help people with mental health problems?

Why People Take Drugs

Any chemicals which have an effect on your mind or body are <u>drugs</u>. That includes caffeine, alcohol and nicotine, <u>as well as</u> illegal drugs like heroin, Es, or speed. People mainly use drugs because they <u>like the effects</u>, but there are <u>other reasons</u> too.

Drugs Change the Way People Feel

<u>All</u> drugs <u>change</u> your body chemistry. A drug will make your <u>body</u> or <u>mind</u> or <u>both</u> feel different. You could even <u>see</u> things differently or see things that <u>aren't there</u>.

<u>Side-effects</u> are a part and parcel of the whole drugs package. As well as the effects you think you <u>want</u> from a drug there are usually <u>nasty side-effects</u> on your mental or physical health — or maybe <u>both</u>.

With <u>alcohol</u>, you pay the price the next morning, in the form of a <u>hangover</u>. With <u>cigarettes</u>, you pay the price every day with steadily deteriorating health and, years later, with <u>lung cancer</u>.

You know Gerry, your body feels somehow different today. I like it.

People Use Drugs for All Sorts of Reasons

Some of the reasons why people use drugs sound quite <u>sensible</u>, others <u>don't</u>.

CURIOSITY They're <u>interested</u> in seeing what different drugs are like.

IMAGE They want to feel <u>older</u>, <u>cooler</u> or <u>harder</u> than other people.

ESCAPISM They have <u>problems</u> they would rather forget about. Drugs are a way of getting temporary <u>time off</u> from their problems.

BOREDOM They're <u>bored</u> and take drugs for a change.

ENJOYMENT They just <u>enjoy</u> the feeling that a drug gives them.

REBELLION They want to <u>test</u> how their parents (or their friends, or their school, or the police...) will react if they <u>do something extreme</u>.

Joining In with Friends Can Be a Big Reason

1) Groups of friends often have the <u>same interests</u> — and <u>similar attitudes</u> to drugs.

2) If your friends are using drugs it might <u>seem</u> better to join in than be <u>left out</u>.

3) People worry that they'll look like they're <u>boring</u> or <u>a chicken</u> if they don't join in.

BUT When you're <u>addicted</u> to a drug, you <u>don't</u> care about other people as much.

Using Illegal Drugs can Ruin your Plans

<u>Remember</u> — you could get <u>found out</u> at any time.

If you have any sort of <u>police record</u> for <u>possessing or supplying drugs</u>, you <u>can't</u> go to the <u>USA</u> — ever. So <u>no Disneyworld</u> then.

You don't have to go to court to get a <u>criminal record</u>. A police <u>caution</u> will go on your <u>record</u> and can stay there for five years. Anyone you apply for a job with can find out about it — and might <u>refuse</u> to <u>employ</u> you.

Change the way you feel — use your toes instead of fingers...

The <u>social pressure</u> to use <u>recreational drugs</u> of one sort or another (including alcohol) is almost inescapable. Certainly, there's <u>fun</u> to be had — no question about that. But there are <u>dangers</u> too. All we can do is give you the <u>facts</u> to help <u>you</u> make good choices — after that it's <u>all up to you</u>.

Nicotine

Loads of people enjoy smoking fags — and often it's glamorous people like film stars, etc.
Whether you smoke already or think you want to — it's a fine idea to know the flip side.

People Start Smoking for Social Reasons

Sometimes people start smoking so that they can get in with other people who smoke.

Some people start smoking because they think it'll make
them look hard and grown-up — less like a kid.

There's a kind of glamour attached to the act of smoking — especially in films.

People Carry On Smoking because...

Smoking certainly helps people cope with stress, much as alcohol (or indeed any drug) does.
People quickly become dependent on the relief (from stress) that it gives them. This is a kind of
mental addiction, and (as with all drugs) that's where the problems lie. But there are other reasons...

1) Some people carry on smoking because they feel that it helps them to concentrate.

2) Some smokers carry on because they feel it calms them down when they're stressed.

3) Some people say smoking reduces their appetite — or maybe it's just something other than
   eating that they can do when they're bored.

4) Smokers enjoy their smoking rituals (e.g. the first cigarette of the morning or tapping the
   cigarette on the table before smoking it) and smoking paraphernalia (e.g. a special lighter or
   tobacco box).

5) Lots of smokers carry on smoking because they've tried to give up before, and didn't like the
   way that giving up made them feel.

There's an Instant Effect From Smoking

Nicotine (the drug in cigarettes) increases heart rate and
blood pressure the instant a smoker takes a first drag.

Smokers feel more relaxed as soon as they take a drag on a cigarette.
If you think about it, this is slightly odd — you'd expect high heart rate
to go with feeling excited or tense, not with feeling calm.

Paul's precious second of relaxation

Smoking is Very Addictive

PHYSICAL ADDICTION

1) The nicotine in tobacco is extremely addictive. A smoker's brain quickly starts to rely on it in
   order to stay calm and carry on a regular life. Some people think that nicotine addiction and
   short term withdrawal cause the stress that cigarette smoking relieves — so it's a vicious circle.

2) When the nicotine is suddenly taken away (e.g. when the smoker tries to give up, or when he or
   she runs out of cigarettes) the smoker can get very short tempered, stressed and ratty.

3) If you spot somebody looking viciously grumpy, and prowling around restlessly for no apparent
   reason, they may well be a smoker gasping for a fag.

MENTAL ADDICTION

1) People just get into the habit of smoking — and all habits can be hard to give up.

2) A smoker only needs about 5 cigarettes a day to satisfy the physical addiction to nicotine.
   Smoking more than that is down to habit (or stress relief), not physical addiction.

Nicotine

Smoking has some long-term <u>health risks</u>. It's worth making yourself aware of them.

Smoking Is a Health Risk

Tar clogs up smokers' lungs — and smoking causes several <u>deadly diseases</u>.

- One in five <u>deaths</u> in Britain is caused by smoking.

- One in two long-term smokers dies <u>prematurely</u>.

- The longer someone is a smoker the <u>worse</u> it is for their body, and the <u>harder</u> it is for them to <u>give up</u>.

- <u>Passive smokers</u> (people who breathe in other people's smoke) damage their health in the <u>same way</u> that smokers do — just not as <u>much</u>. Non-smokers <u>aren't</u> very likely to get <u>lung cancer</u> from passive smoking.

LUNG CANCER
N*i*C*E*
Nasty, Incurable [often], Corrosive & Evil.

MOUTH CANCER
N*i*C*E*
(see lung cancer)

HEART DISEASE

BRONCHITIS
painful hacking cough, thick mucus and swollen membranes (mmmm...tasty).

EMPHYSEMA (a lung disease)
over-inflation of air sacs causes breakdown of lung walls and leaves victim breathless — phew...

Very Heavy Smoking Will Make You Look Rough

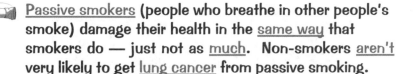

Smoke 20 a day like me, and you too could look this good at the tender age of 21.

Some young people smoke because they reckon smoking is gonna make them look <u>older</u>.
Well, it <u>does</u> — just not quite in the way they expect.

<u>Heavy smoking</u> makes it harder for oxygen to reach the skin cells, so the skin becomes more prone to <u>wrinkling</u>.

Smoking stains your <u>teeth</u> a "fetching" shade of <u>yellow</u>. Unfortunately, brushing doesn't properly get rid of it.

Heavy smoking usually ends up in <u>seriously bad breath</u> and nasty <u>gum disease</u>.

If You Won't Quit — Cut Down on Your Smoking

Healthwise, <u>never</u> having a cigarette and certainly never having two is the <u>best option</u>. But if you're a smoker <u>already</u> and you can't give up, then try <u>cutting down</u>. 3-5 cigarettes a day is going to be <u>easier</u> on your <u>pocket</u> and <u>kinder</u> to your <u>lungs</u> than 20. Common sense, innit.

If you do <u>manage</u> to <u>cut down</u>, then <u>giving up</u> won't be such a <u>mammoth task</u> if you <u>do decide</u> you wanna try it.

No butts — smoking IS dangerous...

Smoking is such a <u>normal</u> everyday thing that it's easy to <u>overlook</u> how big a <u>health risk</u> it is. I wonder why that is... it seems <u>weird</u> that something so risky should be so popular — or is that the point?

Alcohol

Legal Drugs

Alcohol is a lot more <u>socially acceptable</u> then tobacco these days. Even people who don't go out to the pub regularly will quite happily enjoy the odd <u>civilised</u> glass of sherry or wine.

People Drink to Relax or to have a Good Time

Alcohol is a <u>depressant</u> — which basically means it <u>relaxes</u> the body and <u>slows down reactions</u>. That's why it's <u>incredibly dangerous</u> to <u>drive</u> when you're <u>drunk</u>.

How someone <u>reacts</u> to drinking booze — whether they get rowdy or weepy or start singing or whatever — can depend on their <u>state of mind</u> at the time.

Someone in a <u>bad mood</u> drinking to <u>cheer themselves up</u> might find the alcohol actually makes the bad mood even <u>worse</u>.

Some people <u>often</u> react a certain way to alcohol — i.e. they nearly always get jolly or weepy or quiet or rowdy.

Alcohol starts to take effect <u>5-10 minutes</u> after drinking.

It's <u>against the law</u> for <u>under 18s</u> to <u>buy</u> alcoholic drinks, but that doesn't stop most people. Think about this — if you get <u>caught drinking under age</u> in a pub, <u>you'll</u> get <u>fined</u>. It's not only the <u>landlord</u> who suffers.

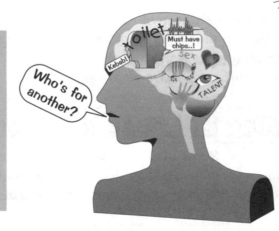

"Life of the Party" effects
- *less inhibited*
- *less coordinated*
- *more relaxed*
- *LOUDER*
- *jollier*

Who's for another?

"Kill-joy" effects
- *more argumentative*
- *more aggressive*
- *more violent*
- *more depressed*

After about <u>8</u> standard glasses of wine, <u>slurring</u>, <u>dribbling</u> and <u>gibbering</u> start to take over.

Being <u>used</u> to drinking, and being able to '<u>hold your drink</u>' doesn't mean you don't <u>actually get drunk</u>. It just means that you're not so <u>obvious</u> about it.

Never underestimate how <u>easy</u> it is for <u>other people</u> to <u>tell</u> you've been drinking. Chewing <u>spearmint gum</u> on the way home and not saying a lot to your folks when you get there <u>won't</u> really cut it.

It's Important to Know How Much You're Drinking

Everyone knows some alcoholic drinks are <u>stronger</u> than others. Drinks that are <u>stronger</u> than you thought will make you <u>much more drunk</u> than you'd planned for — and <u>much faster</u>.

Alcohol <u>messes up</u> your ability to <u>make decisions</u> — including decisions about <u>how much</u> to drink.

Try to keep a <u>rough idea</u> of how many <u>units of alcohol</u> you've had. It helps if you know <u>how many units</u> each type of drink has. For example, <u>strong lager</u> has 3-4 units a pint, and bog standard lager has 2 units a pint. Also remember that you'll pour much <u>bigger measures</u> at home than the ones you get in a pub.

Here are two good ways to stay in control:

1) <u>Stop drinking alcohol</u> and switch to <u>soft drinks</u> if you start to get <u>more drunk</u> than you want to be.

2) <u>Alternate</u> between <u>soft drinks</u> and alcoholic drinks to <u>spread out</u> a <u>small</u> alcohol intake over an evening.

| *Spirits* 30-40% alcohol | *Wine* 10-15% alcohol | *Beer* 3-7% alcohol | *Alcopop* 3-6% alcohol | *Cola* NO alcohol |

Alcohol

Anybody who's ever drunk alcohol probably knows about <u>hangovers</u>.
Drinking alcohol and being drunk have a few other <u>health risks</u> that you should know about.

Being Drunk is a Risky Business

Being drunk makes you more likely to:

1) <u>fall over</u> — this can result in nasty injuries if you fall down stairs, or bash your head, etc.

2) be <u>sexually promiscuous</u> and lose the power of judgement (beer-goggles alert)

3) lose <u>consciousness</u>

4) <u>vomit</u> (violently)

5) get injured or <u>die</u> (in any number of ways, choking on vomit being just one)

Be Prepared — Avoid the Worst of a Hangover

A hangover is caused mostly by <u>dehydration</u> — alcohol "tricks" your body into
<u>getting rid</u> of more water than you should and your body gets slightly <u>dried out</u>
inside because of it. This causes most of the <u>hangover symptoms</u>.

1) <u>Avoid dehydration</u> by <u>drinking</u> a couple of <u>pints of water</u> before passing out.

2) <u>Don't take paracetamol</u> to put off a hangover headache. Alcohol makes
paracetamol a lot more potent — so it's possible to overdose on only a few
tablets. Paracetamol overdoses <u>kill</u> — in a long, drawn out, <u>painful</u> way.

MYTH: coffee does <u>not</u> help you sober up or help rehydrate you. It will just make you <u>wide-awake drunk</u>.

Heavy Long-Term Drinking is Dangerous

<u>Heavy drinking</u> damages
important parts of the body:

drink...
...DRINK!!!

liver gets diseased

brain damage

heart failure

stomach becomes inflamed

People who drink a <u>large amount</u> over a long
time also get <u>fat</u> (the <u>beer belly</u> effect) and their
faces become <u>reddened</u> and a bit <u>puffy</u>.

Heavy drinkers build up their <u>alcohol tolerance</u> at each <u>drinking session</u>. They
need more and more alcohol to feel the same <u>effect</u> — and they start <u>craving</u> it.

<u>Social drinkers</u> can all too easily turn into <u>alcoholics</u>. Alcoholics are <u>physically dependent</u>
— they'll start <u>trembling</u>, <u>sweating</u>, and feeling <u>anxious</u> if they can't have a drink.

Binge Drinking is Foolhardy

The odd drink now and then, or a couple of units of alcohol a night is fine. <u>Binge</u> drinking,
though, is <u>dangerous</u> and foolhardy. Having another drink before the last one's really
taken effect means you'll get a <u>lot more drunk</u> than you're expecting to.
Too much alcohol can <u>kill</u> you — people have actually <u>died</u> after massive drinking sessions.

Alcohol doesn't mix well with other drugs. <u>Mixing</u> drugs and alcohol <u>kills people</u>.

A quick one for the road...

So alcohol's <u>legal</u> — fine. It's also <u>socially accepted</u> — fine. But — alcohol is a dangerous and
<u>addictive</u> substance, with loads of <u>health risks</u> and '<u>idiot behaviour</u>' risks. Definitely handle with care.

Illegal Drugs

Cannabis

Cannabis is <u>illegal</u>, but it's very <u>widely available</u>. Although it used to be linked to <u>hippies</u> in the 60s, it's more of a <u>gangster rap</u> and <u>hip-hop</u> thing nowadays.

Cannabis Makes You Feel Spaced-out

There are lots of <u>different</u> kinds of cannabis which all <u>affect</u> people differently. The way somebody's <u>feeling</u> when they take it is gonna <u>influence</u> the effect — and so will any other drug they've already taken. <u>Hardened</u> users will build up <u>tolerance</u> and need to smoke more to get the same effects.

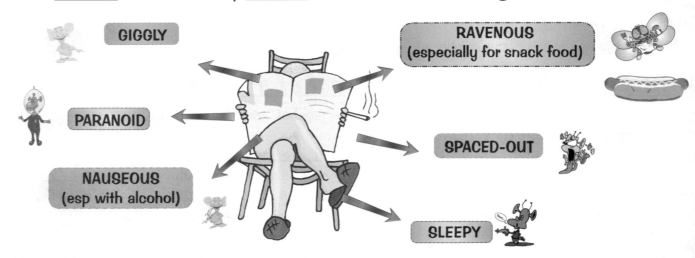

GIGGLY

RAVENOUS
(especially for snack food)

PARANOID

SPACED-OUT

NAUSEOUS
(esp with alcohol)

SLEEPY

Cannabis Isn't Always the First Step to 'Hard' Drugs

<u>Anybody</u> buying cannabis is likely to come into <u>contact</u> with people who sell or use <u>other illicit drugs</u> as well. Because of this, some people say that smoking cannabis is just the first step on the <u>rocky road</u> to full-time drug <u>addiction</u>. This isn't always the case — it <u>can</u> be, but it doesn't <u>follow</u> automatically.

<u>Drug dealers</u> are <u>not always</u> suspect, unemployed, shifty-looking <u>geezers</u>. If they were, the police would be able to <u>spot</u> them and <u>arrest</u> them all. They might well be the kid who lives next door and has <u>loads of mates</u> — or your older sister's <u>posh friend</u>.

<u>Remember</u> — even if somebody is <u>just</u> buying drugs for their friend as a <u>favour</u> and not making <u>profit</u> on it, they are still <u>dealing</u> in the eyes of the <u>law</u>. The penalties for <u>supplying</u> cannabis are <u>much harsher</u> than the penalties for <u>possession</u>.

Cannabis Has Some Serious Health Issues

Cannabis has most of the same <u>health risks</u> as <u>tobacco</u>. It coats the smoker's lungs with thick <u>sticky tar</u> — which causes cancer, just like tar from ordinary cigarettes.

You may have heard <u>stories</u> of people with <u>chronic illnesses</u> using it as a <u>pain killer</u>. This does happen, and people claim it helps them — but remember — whatever it's used for, cannabis is <u>ILLEGAL</u>, and possessing or using it is a <u>prosecutable</u> offence.

Cannabis is a controversial drug...

Alcohol is <u>legal</u> and <u>socially accepted</u>. But look at what it <u>does to people</u> compared to a drug like <u>cannabis</u>... some people say if cannabis is <u>illegal</u>, alcohol <u>should be</u> too. What do <u>you</u> think?

Illegal Drugs

Ecstasy

Ecstasy (E) is a psychedelic stimulant and it's especially dangerous to anybody with a history of mental health problems, or who isn't firmly on the rails.

Ecstasy is a Mood Elevator

Ecstasy is pure MDMA, a 'happy' drug that kicks in 20-40 minutes after being taken and can cause any of these effects:

feelings of affection

wide awake

blissed-out feeling

self confidence

relaxed feeling

Full-on Ecstasy

The Pits

confused

shivering

nauseous

depressed

paranoid

miserable

anxious

Whether they have a good time or a bad time all Ecstasy users experience certain physical effects:

☺ loss of appetite
☺ tight jaw
☺ rise in blood pressure
☺ dilated pupils
☺ bad coordination — can dance, but can't do fiddly things

Some people have died after taking E because they thought they had to drink vast amounts of water. The excess water made their brains swell up. Nasty.

Ecstasy Can result in Bad After-effects

With all drugs, what goes up must come down. The thing is, Ecstasy messes with the brain more than (say) alcohol does. An alcohol hangover makes a drinker feel physically rubbish, but an Ecstasy hangover (or 'comedown') will make the pill-taker feel mentally rotten as well — two for the price of one (grrreat).

What's Sold as Ecstasy Could Be Lethal

Because Ecstasy is an illegal drug nobody can ever be sure what's in the pills they're buying. There are a lot of drug combinations that may be sold as E. Some contain Ecstasy, a lot don't.

1) Pure Ecstasy is unlikely to kill. (It's what people do after they've taken it that could leave them the wrong side of dead.)

2) Anyone taking Ecstasy is taking an illegally produced drug without knowing what's in it. That's one jiggernormously huge risk of poisoning or overdose in the hope of a quick high.

Nobody Knows for Sure what Ecstasy's Long-Term Effects Are

Ecstasy hasn't been on the illicit market long enough for people to be totally sure what the long-term effects of regular use are. But it's been about long enough for us to have a fair idea. So far, it's been linked to depression, anxiety and memory loss.

Not exactly what people have in mind when they decide to take it.

(See P.44 & 45 for more on depression and anxiety.)

Ecstasy — it's a serious risk...

You don't ever know what's in it — that's why ecstasy pills can be deadly. It may only take one pill to kill you... it's a huge mojofunkin gamble. Even pure MDMA has serious long term health risks.

Illegal Drugs

Acid, Mushrooms & Speed

Ecstasy is a combination of hallucinogens and stimulants, so it <u>messes</u> with your <u>brain</u> and keeps your <u>body going</u>. Acid and Magic Mushrooms <u>just</u> mess with your brain, whilst speed just gives you <u>energy</u> — phew...

Acid and Mushrooms *Warp your Picture of the World*

<u>Acid</u> (LSD) and Magic Mushrooms are <u>psychedelic drugs</u> — which means they cause hallucinations. Like groovy man... well, groovy until you start <u>hearing voices</u> and convince yourself that everybody is <u>out to get you</u>.

A small Square of Paper Can *Send You Mad*

Acid is <u>usually</u> supplied on small squares of <u>blotting paper</u> with little pictures of strawberries, or footballs, or anything else printed on them. <u>Magic Mushrooms</u> are usually supplied <u>dried</u> and <u>loose</u>, but may be in <u>capsules</u>. They have the same basic effects as LSD.

② The trip <u>progresses</u> over the next <u>few hours</u> and things start <u>appearing</u> out of <u>thin air</u>.

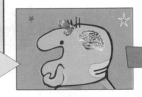

④ The <u>comedown</u> lasts <u>5-6</u> hours and the tripper may well be left feeling <u>uneasy</u> and out of synch for <u>weeks</u> afterwards.

① About <u>half an hour</u> after <u>swallowing</u> acid the user will start to see '<u>trails</u>' on objects and begin to feel the <u>special effects</u> guy in their <u>mind</u> has gone a bit <u>overboard</u>.

③ The '<u>Head Trip</u>' is the most <u>intense</u> bit. Time will <u>seem</u> to <u>stand still</u>, and while some find this mystical and <u>enlightening</u>, it <u>scares</u> others half to death.

If the tripper decides to <u>totally lose it</u> and take loads of acid they'll actually be '<u>psychotic</u>' or '<u>insane</u>' for as long as their '<u>Head Trip</u>' lasts.

Anybody who's a bit <u>mentally wobbly</u> and decides to take a <u>strong</u> trip could well discover they've bought a one way ticket to life in a mental <u>institution</u>. It doesn't happen <u>often</u>, but it does happen.

Speed Gives Your Body an 'Energy Loan'...

Speed (<u>amphetamine</u>) is a <u>white powder</u> sold cut (mixed) with <u>loads</u> of other stuff, like baby milk powder or paracetamol. People take it by <u>sniffing</u> or <u>injecting</u> — both of which are pretty darned <u>dangerous</u> if you don't know what on earth's in it. It can also be <u>swallowed</u>.

People take it because it gives them the <u>energy</u> to keep going.

It's a <u>stimulant</u> which acts on the body's <u>central nervous system</u> kinda like caffeine does, speeding up the <u>heart</u> for example.

It <u>kills</u> all <u>appetite</u> and <u>revs up</u> the body.

...then Demands it Back With Interest

As with <u>all</u> drugs there are serious <u>adverse consequences</u>.

1) <u>Immediate</u> comedown will make you <u>exhausted</u> and <u>depressed</u>.
2) It affects your <u>sleep pattern</u> badly.
3) It's very <u>bad</u> for your <u>liver</u>.
4) <u>Prolonged</u> and <u>regular</u> use can make you <u>twitch</u>, <u>cough</u> and <u>shake</u> — and make your <u>skin</u> look <u>old</u>, <u>grey</u> and <u>saggy</u>.

These drugs fry people's minds...

If you want to stay <u>well grounded</u> avoid the psychedelic drugs. As for <u>speed</u>, you just <u>don't know</u> what's in it. It'll wear you out ten times faster than normal life — there's always a <u>payback</u>.

Heroin, Cocaine & Crack

Illegal Drugs

Heroin (quite rightly) has a terrible image. Cocaine on the other hand is part and parcel of the rich'n'famous lifestyle — but it's not as sophisticated as the hype makes out.

Heroin is Highly Addictive

Stereotypical Heroin Addict

Bad skin covered with acne and boils.

Constipation wearing off with the effects of the heroin.

Unemployed and nicking stuff to get money for next 'hit'.

Shaking & sweating — 8 hours since last 'hit'.

Heroin is a white-ish powder made from the opium poppy. It's a sedative drug which depresses the body's nervous system. It can be injected, sniffed, or heated on foil and the fumes inhaled ('chasing the dragon').

Heroin doesn't necessarily hook everyone the first time they use it, and may well make them puke. People who like the blissed-out high run the risk of becoming addicts.

It only takes a few weeks of heavy, regular use to leave a user psychologically and physically dependent on heroin.

It's easy to take too much — and overdose can mean death.

Trying to Kick a Heroin Habit can be Hell

8-24 hours after their last 'hit' the addict will feel like they are suffering from flu. They'll ache, sweat, have violent diarrhoea, tremble, sneeze, suffer muscle tremors, and have an overwhelming urge to get another 'hit' of heroin.

7-10 days after their last dose of heroin the main symptoms will start to go away.

For **several months** the recovering addict will feel weak and unwell.

Injecting & Sharing Needles is Asking for Trouble

Sharing anybody else's needle to inject drugs is unbelievably stupid — you risk getting HIV or any other disease carried by the blood.

Ooh, can I borrow your needle when you've finished?

One Tuesday, Tina felt like asking for trouble.

Snort Too Much Cocaine and Lo, your Nose Will Collapse

Cocaine is usually supplied as white powder and sniffed up the nose. It's linked with film stars, celebrities and lives of glamour — which means it's expensive and gives a very short lived high.

People who are high on cocaine have a tendency to be arrogant, boring, self-opinionated, self-infatuated etc. That's something to bear in mind if it's popularity you're after.

If you sniff too much coke the cartilage in your nose collapses — leaving you with pretty much no nose. That's, er, "nice".

I've just got to have this nose. It's to die for!

Crack is more Addictive than Plain Cocaine

Cocaine and crack cocaine are both stimulants. Cocaine can be addictive in a psychological way — the high lasts for such a short time that users may find themselves wanting to repeat it, and repeat it, and repeat it...

Crack is a form of cocaine made into crystals and smoked. It's incredibly addictive — far more addictive than cocaine. The comedown is very, very bad.

Large doses, or a quick succession of hits over a short time, of either crack or cocaine, can cause anxiety, paranoia and even hallucinations. There's always the risk of an overdose.

It's not so glitzy when you put it like that...

These are the famous drugs — the ones you hear about on the telly. But they aren't nearly as cool as people make out. It makes you wonder why so many rich and famous people end up hooked on them — maybe their lives aren't as perfect as they seem after all...

Solvents & Other Nasty Narcotics

There are <u>millions</u> of drugs, <u>loads</u>, more than you could shake a <u>very big stick</u> at.
I can't tell you all about all of them, just a bit about some of them.

You Can _Die_ Trying to Get an _Easy High_

DXM (dextromethorphan):

1) It's a psychedelic drug.

2) It's found in some cough medicines — usually with other drugs. These other drugs are very dangerous in large quantities.

3) DXM causes very bad allergic reactions in some people.

4) It can cause mental health problems or fry your brain if it's used a lot.

Solvents:

1) It's <u>illegal</u> for under 18's to buy solvents for the purpose of inhaling them to get high.

2) They affect the brain quickly when inhaled.

3) They make you feel or be sick 9 times out of 10.

4) Solvents make the user pass out if they take too much, then they could choke on vomit (blee).

5) Solvents can cause heart failure and suffocation (that's <u>death</u>, by the way) if squirted straight into the mouth.

Other Drugs are _Very Dangerous_ and _Illegal to Supply_

Prescription drugs can be <u>lethal</u> if they haven't been prescribed for you.

Tranquilisers:

1) Mogadon, Valium, Rohypnol and Temazepam are prescription drugs.

2) They're all very addictive.

3) It's illegal to give prescription drugs to anybody else.

4) Possession of Temazepam or Rohypnol ('date rape' drug) without prescription is illegal.

5) It's easy to overdose on them and die.

GHB (gamma-hydroxybutanol, 'Liquid E'):

1) It's a depressant.

2) Some body builders use it for muscle development.

3) Some clubbers take it to lower inhibitions.

4) It's surprised a fair few users by killing them — the lethal dose is very small, and it doesn't mix AT ALL with booze.

Ketamine (Special K):

1) It's a psychedelic drug.

2) It's a powerful horse anaesthetic — illegal to possess if you're not a vet.

3) Using it can be a very scary experience.

4) It can cause hallucinations, numbness, muscle twitches and puking.

Cocktails are _Incredibly Stupid_

Nope, we're <u>not</u> talking <u>tequila sunrises</u>, I mean <u>mixing drugs</u>.
Mixing drugs is very, very unwise.

Drugs can <u>combine</u> to have some <u>seriously nasty</u> effects,
for example alcohol and paracetamol (see P.53)

Experimenting is extremely dangerous...

It's <u>not OK</u> to take a drug just cos it's legal — it could still do you a lot more <u>harm</u> than good. Taking prescription drugs that <u>weren't</u> prescribed for you is <u>foolhardy</u>, and sniffing solvents <u>makes my skin crawl</u>...

Revision Summary

You may well lead a happy, drug-free existence and never come into contact with illegal narcotics. But you never know who you're going to meet up with in the future — and what influence they might have on you. If you do use illicit drugs or know somebody who does there's always the possibility something could go very wrong. If an emergency comes up, keep your head and make sure you know how to get help.

1) Give four different reasons why people use drugs.

2) Give two examples of ways that illegal drug use can affect your future plans.

3) What are the three main reasons why people start smoking?

4) Give four reasons why smokers carry on smoking rather than giving up.

5) Why do smokers get bad tempered when trying to give up?

6) Why else do smokers find it hard to give up smoking?

7) What are the immediate effects that smoking has on the body?

8) Give three examples of diseases caused by smoking.

9) Why do people drink alcohol?

10) Why is it dangerous to drive when drunk?

11) Does someone with a 'tolerance' for alcohol really get less drunk?

12) Give two examples of ways to avoid getting too drunk when drinking alcohol.

13) Give four examples of bad stuff that can happen to someone because they're drunk.

14) What's a good way to avoid the worst symptoms of a hangover?

15) Is cannabis always the first step on the road to harder drugs?

16) If someone gives you enough cannabis for a joint or two, is that dealing?

17) Can you tell what's in a pill sold as ecstasy?

18) Can acid send you mad?

19) Why are heroin users at risk of catching HIV?

If You Witness an Overdose you have to Act Immediately

If you are ever with somebody taking drugs and things start to go wrong, don't hang around worrying about getting into trouble with the police. Dithering could cost your mate's life, and so could freezing like a rabbit caught in headlights. Phone for an ambulance immediately, or get somebody (sober) to drive you and your mate to the nearest hospital if that'll be faster.

What to look out for varies with different kinds of drugs — whether illegal, prescribed or a mixture. Some of the symptoms of a possible overdose are:

Abnormal breathing	Reddish face
Slurred speech	Heavy sweating
Lack of coordination	Drowsiness
Slow or rapid pulse	Delusions and/or hallucinations
Low or elevated body temperature	Unconsciousness which may lead to coma
Enlarged or small eye pupils	

If your mate has taken an illegal drug and looks seriously ill then tell the doctors exactly what you think they took — if you don't you might lose a mate.

Index

Useful Contacts

We think these phone numbers and websites might come in handy.
Obviously, it's up to you whether you phone them, and whether you take their advice.

Sex

Family Planning Association
  (contraception and sexual health)
  0845 310 1334 (Helpline)
  www.fpa.org.uk

Brook Advisory
  (advice on contraception)
  0800 0185 023
  www.brook.org.uk
  information@brookcentres.org.uk

British Pregnancy Advisory Service
  (all options including abortion)
  08457 30 40 30
  www.bpas.org

Life
  (for adoption or keeping the baby)
  01926 311667
  www.lifeuk.org

Lesbian and Gay Switchboard
  020 7387 7324
  www.llgs.org.uk   admin@llgs.org.uk

Prejudice

Commission for Racial Equality
  www.cre.gov.uk

Equal Opportunities Commission
  (gender)
  www.eoc.org.uk

Britkids
  www.britkid.org

Health and Food

NHS Direct
  0845 46 47
  www.nhsdirect.nhs.uk

Doctor Ann
  (health info and advice)
  website www.doctorann.org

British Nutrition Foundation
  www.nutrition.org

Looking after yourself

Bullying Online
  www.bullying.co.uk
  help@bullying.co.uk

Divorce — BBC Online
  www.bbc.co.uk/education/archive/divorce/index.shtml

National Society for the Prevention of Cruelty to Children
  www.nspcc.org.uk

Shelter (Homelessness advice)
  helpline 0808 800 4444
  info line 020 7505 4699
  www.shelter.org.uk

Mental Health

Mind (mental health charity)
  www.mind.org.uk

Sane (mental health charity)
  Saneline 0845 767 8000
  www.sane.org.uk

Eating disorders support and help
  www.anred.com

Drugs

Trashed
  (drugs info)
  www.trashed.co.uk

Wrecked
  (alcohol info)
  www.wrecked.co.uk

National drugs helpline
  0800 77 66 00 (free, confidential, won't show on bills)
  www.healthwise.org.uk/ndh2.htm

Drinkline
  0808 917 8282

Alateen
  (for teenagers bothered by parent or friend drinking)
  020 7403 0888

Resolve
  0808 800 2345

We don't necessarily agree with all the opinions held by these organisations. We're giving their names because we hope they'll be useful sources of information and help — but we accept no responsibility for any advice they might give you.

Useful Contacts

We think these phone numbers and websites might come in handy.
Obviously, it's up to you whether you phone them, and whether you take their advice.

Urgent help in a crisis

The Samaritans
  phone 08457 90 90 90 (24 hours, confidential)
  jo@samaritans.org
  www.samaritans.org

Childline
  0800 11 11 (free, confidential, doesn't show on bill)
  www.childline.co.uk

and the 'obvious ones'...

Police — dial 999
  In a violent situation, or if your physical safety is under threat, call the
  police. If you see a crime being committed, call the police. If you
  discover a situation where a crime has been committed, call the police.

  Dial 999 in an emergency. If it's not an emergency, call your local police station
  (the phone number's in the ordinary phone book)

Ambulance — dial 999
  If someone has been seriously injured, call an ambulance.

General information

Diary of a Teenage Health Freak
  www.petepayne.com
  www.doctorann.org (Health advice from the fictional Dr Ann on topics from sex to spots)

Web addresses can go out of date quite fast. The bigger
organisations try to make a point of not changing theirs, but
smaller places sometimes have no choice about it. If this book's
been out for a while, some of the web addresses on this page and
the one before might have changed. It's best to do a search for
the organisation's name on a good search engine and check.

We don't necessarily agree with all the opinions held by these organisations. We're giving their names because we hope
they'll be useful sources of information and help — but we accept no responsibility for any advice they might give you.